The K-12
Guidebook

The K-12 Educator's Data Guidebook is a comprehensive field guide for school professionals learning to use data. "Non-data people," rejoice! Requiring no prior proficiency in data tools and programming, this book validates the implicit challenges of learning to use data to empower educators and features original real-world examples from in-service educators to illustrate common problem-solving. Each chapter uses stories, humor, and a human approach to set the tone for a safe and fun learning experience. Through this highly practical foundation, everyday educators can better engage school initiatives, professional development, and instructional challenges that require competent data use for improving school systems.

Ryan A. Estrellado is Executive Consultant and Program Administrator at the South County Special Education Local Plan Area of the San Diego County Office of Education, USA. He is the co-author of *Data Science in Education Using R*, an innovative open-source book about learning data science using real-life education data. A writer, educator, and data scientist, Ryan has over twenty years of experience in public education. He lives with his family in San Diego, CA.

Other Eye on Education Books Available From Routledge
(www.routledge.com/k-12)

Teaching in the Game-Based Classroom:
Practical Strategies for Grades 6–12
David Seelow

What to Look for in Literacy: A Leader's Guide to
High Quality Instruction
Angela Peery and Tracey Shiel

Building Effective Learning Environments:
A Framework for Merging the Best of
Old and New Practices
Kevin S. Krahenbuhl

The Brain-Based Classroom: Accessing Every Child's
Potential Through Educational Neuroscience
Kieran O'Mahony

Thriving as an Online K-12 Educator: Essential Practices
from the Field
Jody Peerless Green

The Media-Savvy Middle School Classroom:
Strategies for Teaching Against Disinformation
Susan Brooks-Young

The K-12 Educator's Data Guidebook

Reimagining Practical Data Use in Schools

Ryan A. Estrellado

Routledge
Taylor & Francis Group

NEW YORK AND LONDON

Cover Image Credit: Getty Iimages

First published 2022
by Routledge
605 Third Avenue, New York, NY 10158

and by Routledge
4 Park Square, Milton Park, Abingdon, Oxon, OX14 4RN

*Routledge is an imprint of the Taylor & Francis Group,
an informa business*

Library of Congress Cataloging-in-Publication Data
A catalog record for this book has been requested

ISBN: 978-0-367-68718-2 (hbk)
ISBN: 978-0-367-68948-3 (pbk)
ISBN: 978-1-003-13975-1 (ebk)

DOI: 10.4324/9781003139751

Typeset in Palatino
by Apex CoVantage, LLC

To Santos and Sylvia, the best brunch crew I could ever wish for, even during a year of no brunches.

Contents

Meet the Author

Ryan A. Estrellado is a writer, educator, and data scientist. He is the co-author of *Data Science in Education Using R*, an innovative open-source book about learning data science using real-life education data. He wrote *The K-12 Educator's Data Guidebook: Reimagining Practical Data Use in Schools* to humanize, challenge, and reframe how data is used in education.

Ryan tells inspiring stories about the reality of education work, ranging from overcoming a fear of data to finding a creative practice in the workplace. He has given talks on delivering compelling data stories, sharing complex topics with broad audiences, and promoting equity in schools. Ryan is a co-host of the podcast About Practice, a show about research and practice in education. He sends free resources for educators in his subscriber email, which you can sign up for at ryanestrellado.com.

Ryan has over twenty years of experience in public education, first as a school psychologist, then as an administrator, and now as a designer and consultant for equity-related projects. Currently, he is Executive Consultant and Program Administrator at the South County Special Education Local Plan Area of the San Diego County Office of Education. He is an alumnus of the Strategic Data Project, a project of the Center for Education Policy Research at Harvard University.

Ryan lives with his family in San Diego, California.

Preface

My wife and I have a data routine we've been doing for years. It starts when I read something about data that gets me really excited—a new statistical technique, a research finding, or a data story.

On occasion, what I've just read is so inspiring that I can't help but share with her. I run to my wife and ask a question I know the answer to and yet ask anyway. Something like, "Have you seen how they use Monte Carlo simulations to predict election results?" My wife's response sets a clear boundary: "No, and also you don't have to explain it."

Sometimes I negotiate. "I can summarize it really well." Without turning her attention away from the task I'd just interrupted, she silently raises her hand. I return to my reading.

At first, I thought this playful exchange happens because I am a data person and she is not. But eventually I saw how wrong I was.

During a blistering hot summer in June, my wife and I noticed the condenser unit of our air conditioner making strange noises. Instead of droning with the usual low hum, it made loud rhythmic noises. Something was definitely wrong.

So we started a thoughtful debate. I argued we should wait until the unit stopped working completely, then replace it. She argued for repairing it to see how long we could keep it going.

A few days later, my wife started the debate again, but with new ammunition. She had collected research articles demonstrating the dangerous effects of high temperatures on pets and projections of that summer's high temperatures. She was a data person.

See, the unasked question that sparks the playful banter with my wife is not "Are you a data person?" It's "Is this data practical for you as a person?" I started writing this book because I wanted to help educators use data more practically. What I learned along the way is that educators can only do that if they repair their relationship with data.

In this book, you'll find stories, practical advice, new perspectives to try on, and a safe way to learn and discover what practical data means for you. The story is told in four parts.

First, you'll learn how to reclaim your relationship with data. In this part, you'll read stories about how our systems influence the way we think of data and how we can think about it in more productive and personal ways.

Second, I'll introduce you to your very own data field guide so you can go into the field ready to identify and use the data you find in the wild. You'll cultivate confidence in your practical data use by learning how to interpret and talk about it.

In the third part, you'll learn techniques for using data. In the process, you'll discover straightforward ways to connect practical data use with the realities of *your* education job.

And in the fourth and final part, you'll learn how using data in novel ways sustains your data use, keeps it practical, and deepens your connection with it.

I wrote this book for you. Keep it in your briefcase or at your desk at the office. Scribble in it, dog ear the pages. Heck, write your data to-do list in the margins. This book and the journey within are yours. Because in the end, practical is personal.

Four Ways to Use Your Guidebook

Read this book how you like. But if you need inspiration, here are four ways to consider:

Jump Right to the Activities

Are you feeling pressed for time? Are you worried you won't get anything out of this book unless you spend hours with it? Start by reading an activity and trying it. You'll find activities at the end of each chapter and you'll find more in the appendix. These activities will empower you to try something new with whatever time you have. And if you do that regularly, you'll discover practicality, one activity at a time.

Jump Right Into the Stories

Do you think of yourself as "not a data person" or "not a numbers person?" Are you worried you won't connect with the ideas in this book? Try flipping through the chapters and looking for stories. I included stories from educators like you plus a few of my own. I hope you see yourself in these stories and I hope they spark something that puts you on the path to practical data use.

Flip Through the Book as Daily Data Problems Arise

If you are the most time-strapped of educators, this method is for you. Keep *The K-12 Educator's Data Guidebook* at the office. When you're feeling stuck with your data or need an activity for an upcoming meeting, use the book as your go-to reference. Flip through the table of contents to find a perspective or activity to get you unstuck. Since many chapters can be read in twenty minutes or less, you're bound to find some inspiration.

Read the Book Cover to Cover

The final method is for the completist. If you're the type of reader who can't stand to leave material unread, read this book cover to cover. When you do this, you'll see the big picture—how the technical combines with the emotional and how the stories combine with the numbers. Practical data use is not discovered in a vacuum. It's influenced by your passions, your job duties, and the systems you work in. Read the whole book and discover that larger context.

So pour yourself a cup of coffee, keep your mind open, lead with your curiosity and get started. It's time to discover what practical data use means for you.

Acknowledgements

Thank you to my best friend and wife, Lucy, and my sons Adam and Dylan. Y'all are my family, team, support network, teachers, and inspiration.

I'm grateful to the DSIEUR team, Emily Freer, Isabella Velásquez, Jesse Mostipak, and Joshua Rosenberg for helping me prove to myself I could write books.

To Cohort 11 and all the members of the Strategic Data Project at the Center for Education Policy Research at Harvard University. You created a community where I can learn and feel at home in my interests.

Thank you to Heather Michel, for being a thoughtful guide while I found my way writing this book.

Sending gratitude to the team at the South County SELPA for all their moral support and encouragement.

Thank you to all the inspiring educators who shared their stories with me, allowed me to share them with others, read chapters, and gave me feedback on the work:

Susan Barrett, Dr. Erin E. Dare, Sylvia Echeverria, Stephanie Evergreen, Santos Gonzalez, Graciela Flores, Megan Grannan, Patricia Hershfeldt, Daniel Jarratt, Arpi Karapetyan, Sean Lara, Julie McLeod, Brennan McMahon Parton, Heather Michel, Briana Richardson, Alex Rosas, Joshua Rosenberg, Donna Santini, Matthew R. Tessier, Ed.D., Judi Vanderhaar, PhD, Isabella Velásquez, Krista Verardo, and Tasha A. Woods.

And last but not least, thank you to Daniel Schwartz at Routledge for all his guidance through this project and with my writing.

—August 2021

Part 1
You and Data
A Relationship

When I was in high school, I joined the cross-country team. For the uninitiated, cross-country is a running sport in which, as the name suggests, participants race over long distances. There was very little that was pleasant about this to me. Eight mile runs in the heat, out-of-breath conversations with teammates, getting yelled at by coaches who were doing something other than running—it wasn't for me.

Not surprisingly, as I got older my distaste for cross-country grew to include exercise in general. The thought of going to the gym conjured thoughts of long runs in overly short shorts, baking in the dry Sacramento heat.

Then one day in my late thirties, I discovered road cycling. I found all kinds of things to enjoy in my new hobby: caring for the trusty carbon fiber steed that was my bicycle, rides with friends, and a commitment to my health and wellness.

But cycling is not all that different from cross-country running. They both require consuming sugar (yay) and they both regularly bring you to your physical and mental limits (boo). So why did I enjoy one and not the other? I realized it wasn't the activity itself, but my relationship with it that created meaning.

And so it is the same with how we use data in schools. How we think about data—what it is and what it should be—creates a relationship with it. Before we dive into the technical part of using data in schools, we need to understand this relationship.

DOI: 10.4324/9781003139751-1

Read this if:

- ◆ You worry that data in schools has become more about numbers and less about people
- ◆ You want to use data more, but worry you won't have time to learn
- ◆ You don't know where you fit into the data culture of your school

Activities in This Section

You'll find these activities at the end of each chapter in this section:

1. Reflecting on Your Data Skills.
2. Imagine the Perfect Test.
3. Making Your Data Meetings Safe.
4. Organize, Learn, and Scale.

Discovering Your Data Gifts

In This Chapter

In this chapter we'll

- ◆ Expand our ideas about ourselves as data users
- ◆ Explore the skills we need to use data practically (spoiler alert: we all have some)
- ◆ Use an activity to identify our data skills

Suggested Reflection

As you read this chapter, make the learning personal by answering these questions:

- ◆ How might you expand your ideas about data beyond end-of-year testing scores?
- ◆ What non-technical skills do you bring to a conversation about education data?

DOI: 10.4324/9781003139751-2

◆ Who are teammates you can partner with on your journey towards practical data use?

In 2010, a software designer named Robin Barooah decided to stop drinking coffee.[1] While some might brave the coffee headaches and quit cold turkey, Barooah was on a different path. Over the next few months, he reduced his coffee intake every week by a tiny amount—20 milliliters to be exact—until he was left with just a sip in his daily cup and then finally, nothing.

Barooah's method for quitting coffee was an extremely practical use of data. How did he know he was reducing his weekly coffee intake uniformly?[2] He measured the amount of coffee he removed from his mug. How did he know he'd nearly eliminated coffee from his morning routine? He saw a coffee cup with 1 milliliter of coffee.

There's another lesson in Barooah's story, and it's one we'll come back to in different ways throughout the book: practical data use is practical because it's personal. Barooah chose a measurement—the amount of coffee in his daily cup—because it *assisted a goal that was important to him.*

For us educators, there's a very similar idea: we make school data practical when we use it to assist goals that are important to us.

And to begin imagining the connection between data and our goals, we need to expand our definition of school data.

It's Not Just Test Scores

For many of us, the words "school data" are synonymous with end-of-year testing data. This kind of data is practical for some educators and not practical for others. It all depends on the job duties and key decisions they encounter every day.

If you are a district office or county level administrator whose job is to guide school improvement, end-of-year testing may very well be a practical dataset. On the other hand, if you are a teaching coach whose job is to collaborate with teachers for instructional improvement, you'll need more than end-of-year testing data to get the job done.

Here's another example. I started my career in education as a school psychologist. End-of-year testing data did not assist the decisions that were important to my job duties. Data like psychoeducational assessment scores, student observation notes, and academic goal progress, did.

As we'll explore throughout this book, connecting data use to our everyday work is a key ingredient in making data meaningful. This looks different for everyone. But when we don't make that connection, resentment towards data can set in. One teacher put it this way: "I'm barely a teacher anymore. Instead I'm a data-hustling 'facilitator,' which is not what is needed. It produces lots of numbers, but not so much learning."[3]

If you feel like this, don't despair. We'll be exploring all kinds of ways to establish a meaningful connection with data use, no matter what your job is in education. And you can start right now by asking yourself "What data supports my decisions at work?" When you answer that question, you take the first big step towards the kind of practical data use Robin Barooah used to stop drinking coffee.

It's Not Just About Technical Skills

Early in my career, my co-workers started calling me a "data person." They've called me that for so long, I started calling myself that too. I'd go to meetings and when people started talking about data I'd say, "I get it. I'm a data person." And folks nodded their heads as if to say, "Ah, he's a data person."

From my point of view, there are two problems with the phrase "data person." First, I think what people actually mean is "technical person." But using data in practical ways requires more than fancy technology. It requires expertise in your education craft, self-awareness, communication, writing, and a spirit of experimentation.

Second, the phrase "data person" implies the existence of the opposite: a "non-data person." The idea of a non-data person suggests a person who cannot learn and grow. Believing that practical data use is some inherent human quality will make it difficult to improve one's relationship with it. Believing that practical data use can be discovered and shaped into a meaningful experience opens up space for all kinds of wonderful possibilities.

You may not enjoy statistics or spreadsheets and that's ok. Lots of people don't enjoy those things. You can still learn to use data practically if you're not a spreadsheet jockey.

It's Not Just Individual Work

I know what it's like to feel doubt about learning to use education data. I tend to feel doubt more intensely when I believe I'm doing this work alone. To explain more, here's a story about imposter syndrome, that feeling that people get when they doubt their skills and worry that, sooner or later, others will find out they don't know what they're doing.

In 2019, I started my journey as a fellow at the Strategic Data Project, a program of the Center for Education Policy Research at Harvard University. This was my first formal training in using education data. Up until that moment, I learned on my own and from anyone in the data science community who was generous enough to help me. After four years of stumbling and hacking my way through my learning journey, I was about to meet up with the country's best education data practitioners. Talk about imposter syndrome!

I landed in Massachusetts feeling my self-doubt pretty hard. But as the group sessions and activities rolled on against the backdrop of a cold Cambridge fall, I saw something I didn't expect to see. Our Strategic Data Project cohort were not individuals that were exceptionally good at every data skill. Instead, we were a collection of people with different and complementary data skills.

Here's the valuable lesson I learned: the way we use data in schools should be a collective effort.[4] We can support each other in discovering the gifts we each bring to our school's data culture. Then we can combine those gifts to improve that data culture.

It's a little like me and cooking. It's true that I won't be making a soufflé any time soon, at least not one people would eat. But there are so many things I can do in the kitchen that are practical, enjoyable, and a contribution to the eating experience at my house. I can make pasta, cook a decent ribeye, scramble eggs, make oatmeal, and toast bread. I acknowledge that this list is embarrassingly short and also mostly breakfast foods. But the point is, I can play on the team with the skills I have.

Imagining the Data Dream Team

People look out the window and daydream about all kinds of things: the perfect island vacation, the perfect dinner, or the perfect career. When I look out my window, I daydream about the perfect school data team. What would that look like? Here are five people I imagine on the school data dream team.

As you read this, ask yourself: Which are you? Which do you want to be?

> **School Systems Specialist**: This is someone who has broad knowledge about the K-12 education system. They know how districts and schools work—especially how and when systems change.
> **Niche Content Specialist**: This is someone who's using their education career to develop a specialty in an area. This person has theoretical and practical knowledge of a topic like math instruction, social emotional learning, or universal design for learning.
> **Researcher**: This person knows how to find, read, process, and summarize high quality research about a given topic.

They also have a knack for drawing themes from multiple sources of information.

Tools Specialist: This person uses software to answer data questions. This is the "doing" part of data analysis.[5] For example, after the team decides they need to know the rate of attendance for the last five years, the tools specialist finds the data, runs the calculations, and visualizes it using software.

Storyteller: And finally, there's the storyteller. This person distills the findings down to a simple, relatable, and human story that connects data points with imagery from real life. They view stories the way Brené Brown does: "Stories are data with a soul."[6]

This dream team is not a formula. There are skills I might have missed. And certainly a team can use data well while missing some of these skills. Or maybe the team is made up of two people, each having multiple data skills. However you imagine your data dream team, this is the takeaway: you have a role to play.[7]

Whatever your gifts, bring them to this team. And if your school or district doesn't have a data team? Find a few like-minded colleagues to start talking and learning about data together.

Some of my best partnerships for data use have been unofficial—just two or more educators who want to learn how to use data better in our jobs.

Conclusion

How we think about data in schools can empower us to use it more practically, or it can hold us back. In this chapter, we challenged ideas about what it means to be a "data person."

When we challenge ideas about data that hold us back, we can replace them with stories about data that empower us to use it practically. Let's explore this further in the next chapter, where we'll discuss a source of data that everyone's got an opinion about.

Activity: Reflecting on Your Data Skills

What This Does
In this activity, you'll identify your strongest area of practical data use.

How This Helps Us
There are important data analysis skills beyond being a spreadsheet wizard. A team that uses a variety of data skills will discover ways to use data that help them make the decisions that are important to students. When each team member reflects on what they bring to a school's data culture, they take the first step towards seeing that practical data use is best done as a team.

Instructions
Rate yourself on each of the following questions. This quiz isn't based on hard science, but it will help you reflect on your strengths.

For each of the questions below, rate yourself on a scale of 1–5:

1 = Strongly disagree, 2 = Disagree, 3 = Neither agree nor disagree, 4 = Agree, 5 = Strongly agree

School Systems Specialist
_____ I know how to roll out a school-wide initiative.

_____ I can facilitate goal-oriented meetings effectively.

_____ I can tell when a project is moving too fast or too slow.

_____ Total

Niche Content Specialist

_____ I'm the go-to person in a particular subject area.

_____ I'm the go-to person in a particular instructional technique.

_____ I tend to go deep on a topic, instead of learning broadly across topics.

_____ Total

Researcher

_____ I regularly read research articles.

_____ I know how to find research articles on an education topic.

_____ I know how to access research articles on an education topic.

_____ Total

Tools Specialist

_____ I know how to use spreadsheet tools like Google Docs or Microsoft Excel.

_____ I understand basic summary statistics like mean, median, mode, and standard deviation.

_____ I can make plots like bar charts or line plots from datasets.

_____ Total

Storyteller

_____ I can identify the essential elements of complex ideas.

_____ I can communicate abstract concepts through real life examples.

_____ I can see connections between stories

_____ Total

Calculate the total for each area. Now you should have enough information to discuss with teammates about which area or areas you feel strong in, and which area or areas you have less experience in. Schedule a time to meet and discuss your results with teammates.

Notes

1. Wolf, Gary. "The Data-Driven Life." The New York Times, 28 April 2010, www.nytimes.com/2010/05/02/magazine/02self-measurement-t.html. Accessed 3 April 2021.
2. This is called a process measure. Process measures don't give you information about the desired outcome. They give you information about the behaviors that lead to the desired outcome. For more, see Bryk, Anthony S., et al. *Learning to Improve: How America's Schools Can Get Better at Getting Better*. Harvard Education Publishing, 2015.
3. thebroadwayflyer. "First day back and I am FED UP with data-driven instruction. (Rant below)." *Reddit*, www.reddit.com/r/Teachers/comments/2rglo2/first_day_back_and_i_am_fed_up_with_datadriven/. Accessed 3 April 2021.
4. Berinato, Scott. "Data Science and the Art of Persuasion." *Harvard Business Review*, January 2019, https://hbr.org/2019/01/data-science-and-the-art-of-persuasion. Accessed 3 April 2021.
5. In my experience, this is the role we associate with the "data person." But it's only one part of a good data team culture.
6. Brené, Brown. "Trust in Emergence: Grounded Theory and My Research Process." *Brené Brown*, https://brenebrown.com/the-research. Accessed 1 April 2021.
7. I'm focusing on how you can contribute to a team, but there's also research about how data teams should function. For more structured approaches and best practices for district and data school teams see Geier, Robb, et al. "District Data Teams: A Leadership Structure for Improving Student Achievement." *PCG Education*, 2012, www.publicconsultinggroup.com/media/1623/edu_district_data_teams_white_paper.pdf. Accessed 3 April 2021;

Hanover Research. "Best Practices for Data Facilitators and Data Teams." 2017, www.antiochschools.net/cms/lib/CA02209771/ Centricity/Domain/43/Assessment%20Documents/Best%20 Practices%20for%20Data%20Facilitators%20and%20Data%20Teams. pdf. Accessed 3 April 2021.

2

Why Tests Aren't Enough

In This Chapter

In this chapter we'll explore why we should expand our definition of school data beyond end-of-year testing.

Suggested Reflection

As you read this chapter, reflect on the following questions:

+ How much do I use end-of-year tests in my instructional planning, if at all?
+ If end-of-year testing were the only data I used to plan instruction, what about my students' learning would I be missing?
+ If end-of-year testing were the only data I used to plan instruction, what about my students' stories would I be missing?
+ What data sources outside of end-of-year testing give me a fuller picture of my students?

DOI: 10.4324/9781003139751-3

In 2001, Santos got her teaching credential. As a newly minted teacher, her first job was at a charter school in her home state, California.

While Santos was launching her teaching career, the United States government created a new law meant to improve schools through, among other things, state-designed tests. The No Child Left Behind (NCLB) Act of 2001 would influence how educators like Santos would come to think about learning, teaching, and data.[1]

In this chapter, we'll learn more about Santos's journey. We'll also explore what happens when we expand our definition of data beyond end-of-year tests.

How Procedures Influence Our Data Use

The first part of this story is about how policies and procedures influence the way we think about practical data use. Sometimes this happens in small ways. For example, consider how work changes for the front desk staff at a school when the enrollment forms they've been using for five years changes.

Other times, it's large-scale policies that influence how we work. The No Child Left Behind Act of 2001 is an example of this. That's because NCLB's requirements focused on showing school improvement through tests. The law made yearly testing a requirement. It also set a goal for all students to be proficient in reading and math. How would educators know when students were proficient in reading in math? The yearly state test results were the required evidence.

For the purposes of our discussion, it's important to note the consequences for schools if they didn't meet the goals set out by NCLB. This is not a comprehensive review of the policy, but it gives us a sense of the stakes.[2]

Schools that didn't meet test score goals would have to pay for their students to attend a different school. Schools that continued to fall short of the test score goals would go through "restructuring." Restructuring could include replacing staff. It could also mean another agency taking over leadership of the school.

For example, between 2000 and 2015, an estimated 160 schools in the Chicago Public Schools system were "closed, phased out or consolidated," according to an article from the National Education Association.[3]

The bottom line is this: testing became a big deal in the early 2000s. It was no longer just a measurement tool. It became a significant factor in running schools. In some cases, it was a factor in a school's continued existence.

This had strong implications for how educators thought about data. To quote education historian and author Diane Ravitch, "Because test scores were the ultimate judge of a school's success or failure, they became more than a measure; they became the purpose of education."[4]

School Quality, Tests, and Teaching

Around the time Santos started teaching, test results became linked to the public perception of the school's quality.[5] This mattered because end-of-year tests were based on state standards for learning. And state standards for learning drove what teachers taught students. Consequently, the content of tests influenced what teachers taught.

At first, Santos and her teammates used the new federal requirements to spark intentional thinking and planning of daily instruction. They started learning more about the material prioritized in the test so they could align their instruction with end-of-year testing.

When Santos and I talked, she shared more about this:

We'd go through the framework of the test. Each standard was weighted by how often they appeared on the test. Ten questions for this standard. Three for this standard.

Two for this other standard. We called the most frequently appearing ones 'power standards.' We'd focus on teaching and assessing the power standards.

This part of Santos's journey shows how educators related to data during the NCLB era. They saw data as a way to pick content to teach, not as a way to measure what *they* picked to teach.

When we decide what to teach by looking at what tests measure, we limit our ability to address all of what our students need. But as we'll see in a moment, Santos's story also shows us that we can reimagine our relationship with data so it puts us back in the driver's seat.

Before we go there, we'll need to unpack the nature of standardized testing so we can better understand their limits. And to do that, we'll need to talk about my annual doctor's visits.

The Problem With Single Measures

Once a year, I get a blood test as part of a checkup with my doctor. It's what happens when you get to my age and have a handful of bad genes. I dread these blood tests. Between the needles and the results (the results! What will they show this year?), there's a fair amount of hand wringing leading up to my appointment.

After a few years of this routine, I had a realization. When I fixate on the yearly blood test, I stress over that one metric. But when I fixate on my health throughout the year, I look at several things for practical decision-making, like my weight, my food journal, the amount of exercise I get every week, and my blood pressure. This collection of data points gives me information about my health, broadly speaking. I feel more informed when I decide what to eat, how much to sleep, and if I'm working too hard. And in the end, these good decisions tend to be the ones that lead to decent blood test results anyway.

Here's the challenge with blood tests—the results can only tell me part of my health story. That's because they can only measure one aspect of my health. And while that aspect of my health is important, I don't define my well-being only by the things measured on a blood test.

So how do I use blood tests practically? I interpret only what they are meant to measure. I can learn about blood sugar levels and cholesterol, but I can't learn about my mental health, my relationships with loved ones, my blood pressure, and countless other things that are important to me.

To be clear, we should all listen to medical professionals for *actual* health advice, not me. But the blood test analogy helps us unpack practical and impractical ways to use a single measure.

For example, yearly standardized tests are expertly designed to take a sample of what students learned by way of a single test at the end of the year.[6] But, like the blood test, they measure very specific things. They should be interpreted within the scope of those things (Figure 2.1).[7]

Tests Only Sample a Bigger Picture

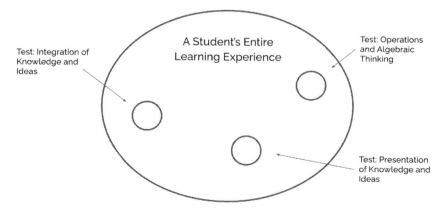

FIGURE 2.1 Tests, by their nature, can only measure samples of what a student learns. To get a holistic sense of a student's learning, educators need to include other sources of data in their work.

When our practical data use only involves end-of-year tests, we miss opportunities to observe and report on any number of measurements that help us create the school experience we want for students. We disconnect the use of data from its ideal purpose—to tell the story of the students we seek to serve.

During Santos's first years of teaching, identifying power standards in the end-of-year test and prioritizing those in lessons felt like the right thing to do. Yearly improvement on test scores signaled a quality education to the school community's families. This was especially meaningful in communities like the one Santos taught in, which had less resources than more affluent areas.

And yet over time this approach felt incomplete to Santos: "I began to see what was wrong. Our conversations reduced our teaching down to only the content that would give our school the most growth on test scores. This approach was taking the focus away from what our students were learning."

Santos never left end-of-year tests out of her planning. They had a part to play in the big picture. But she improved her craft by focusing on what her students needed. Her teaching included the standards covered in the test, but weren't *limited* to those standards.

An Example of What's Missing

I want to take a brief detour here to share an example of something that goes missing when yearly testing is our main source of data. It's a story about Sonya Romero-Smith, a kindergarten teacher in Albuquerque, New Mexico.[8]

Every morning, Sonya greets her students while assessing their well-being. She checks to make sure they've eaten and their clothes are clean. Sonya stocks wipes and fresh socks in her classroom, for days her students need them. The majority of Sonya's students are living in poverty. These daily checks on their well-being are essential to making her students feel safe in the classroom.

In 2018, about 1 out of every 6 students in the United States was living in poverty like the students in Sonya's classroom.[9] The life experiences of students living in poverty differ from those who are not living in poverty.[10] Teachers like Sonya adapt the environment of their classroom so it feels safe. When it feels safe, students are more available for learning.[11] And when they're available for learning, they've got a fair shot of reaching their potential.

Explore this idea with this quick exercise: think of a student you know well who's had a great experience in school, whatever that means to you. Make a list of five things this student experienced to make their experience great. Be sure to include both academic and social descriptions.

Next, think of an assessment this student took at school. It could be an end-of-year test or it could be a weekly quiz. Make a list of five things this assessment measured.

Finally, compare your two lists. How much overlap is there from one list to the other? How much could you depend on that single test to unfold the full story of what learning is like for the student you imagined?

Sonya's story points to possibilities for expanding our data use beyond end-of-year tests. Her daily checks with students are valuable experiences because they guide Sonya to the data sources that matter for her students.

When I imagine Sonya at a school data meeting, I like to think she would present end-of-year test scores from her classroom or grade level alongside poverty data for their school community. And I imagine her weaving stories about her daily checks into her data sharing.

The testing data, community data, and stories come together to present a picture that can lead Sonya and her teammates towards nuanced interventions for their students—and it's all guided by Sonya's experience with them. This kind of picture is a lot harder to uncover with just the end-of-year tests, or with any single measurement.

Conclusion

Applying the scientific method to the decisions we make in schools—what we teach, how we grade, and the interventions we try—is closer to the social sciences than it is to the hard sciences. It's more like sociology than it is biology. There are countless social factors to consider in school data and it's dangerous to draw conclusions without nuance.

To base our decisions on a single data source is to deny the complexity and humanity of the students we seek to serve. As practical data users, we cannot stop the use of standardized tests in the accountability process. But we can understand how these tests work, what they tell us, and their limitations to tell the whole story.

When we acknowledge these limitations, we can harness the strengths of these tests and get value from them. And more importantly, we can start searching for data that help us with the actual decisions we need to make for students. Searching for these sources of data is not only practical, it honors the richness of our students' stories.

After her time in the classroom, Santos went on to lead school sites as a principal. Using data in the No Child Left Behind era clarified her world view. Instruction was a mission and data was a tool for that mission. She chose to see the complex nature of instruction and measurement. And in doing so, she chose to measure the experiences of her students in a way that included, but was not limited by, a single end-of-year test.

Instead of looking for what her students needed to do well on a test, Santos began to look for what they needed to learn in school. Near the end of our interview, Santos told me, "I can't look at a student who's living in a car and tell them they have to do well on a test. They can't read and that's not ok. Reading is thinking."

Data use becomes practical when it approximates the complex experience of students in our classroom and the vision we have for their learning. But students aren't the only people affected by how we use data. In the next chapter, we'll explore the way data use affects us as educators.

Activity: Imagine the Perfect Test

What This Does
In this activity, you'll imagine the elements of the perfect school experience for your students. You'll expand your view of what you want for students beyond the content of end-of-year tests.

How This Helps Us
On an individual level, this activity helps us clarify the experience we want for our students in our classrooms. On a team level, this activity provides a setting where we can share ideas with our teammates.

Instructions
   ♦   List three academic goals you want for your students by the end of the year.
   ♦   For each item, write how you'd know those goals were achieved. Some examples include: students will tell me _____. Parents will tell me _____. Average quiz scores will show me _____.
   ♦   Take note of when end-of-year test scores give us information about the items on our list. Take note of when they don't.

Notes

1. Ravitch, Diane. *The Death and Life of the Great American School System: How Testing and Choice Are Undermining Education*. Basic Books, 2010.
2. For the sake of brevity, I don't go into all the consequences required by NCLB. If you're interested, there's an informative

chapter about this in Ravitch, Diane. The Death and Life of the Great American School System: How Testing and Choice Are Undermining Education. Basic Books, 2010.

3. Rosales, John. "Closing Schools: Privatization Disguised as 'Accountability.'" *National Education Association*, 15 December 2015, www.nea.org/advocating-for-change/new-from-nea/closing-schools-privatization-disguised-accountability. Accessed 5 June 2021.

4. If you can't already tell, I found Ravitch's book extremely informative. Ravitch, Diane. The Death and Life of the Great American School System: How Testing and Choice Are Undermining Education. Basic Books, 2010.

5. Jacobsen, Rebecca, et al. "Informing or Shaping Public Opinion? The Influence of School Accountability Data Format on Public Perceptions of School Quality." *American Journal of Education*, vol. 121, no. 1, 2014.

6. Designing a standardized test well is difficult because test authors have to approximate a large amount of learning with a limited number of test questions. Popham, James W. "Why Standardized Tests Don't Measure Educational Quality." *Using Standards and Assessments*, 1999, www.ascd.org/publications/educational-leadership/mar99/vol56/num06/Why-Standardized-Tests-Don%27t-Measure-Educational-Quality.aspx. Accessed 6 April 2021.

7. Popham, James W. "Why Standardized Tests Don't Measure Educational Quality." Using Standards and Assessments, 1999, www.ascd.org/publications/educational-leadership/mar99/vol56/num06/Why-Standardized-Tests-Don%27t-Measure-Educational-Quality.aspx. Accessed 6 April 2021.

8. Layton, Lyndsey. "Majority of U.S. Public School Students Are in Poverty." *Washington Post*, 16 January 2015, www.washingtonpost.com/local/education/majority-of-us-public-school-students-are-in-poverty/2015/01/15/df7171d0-9ce9-11e4-a7ee-526210d665b4_story.html. Accessed 16 January 2015.

9. This was a national rate. Rates from state to state differed. Institute of Education Sciences, National Center for Education Statistics. "Characteristics of Children's Families." https://nces.ed.gov/programs/coe/indicator_cce.asp. Accessed 12 April 2021.

10. Parrett, William, and Kathleen Budge. "How Does Poverty Influence Learning?" Edutopia, 13 January 2016, www.edutopia. org/blog/how-does-poverty-influence-learning-william-parrett-kathleen-budge. Accessed 13 April 2021.
11. Vogel, Susanne, and Lars Schwabe. "Learning and Memory Under Stress: Implications for the Classroom." *Science Learning*, no. 1, 2016.

3

Rewriting Your Data Story

In This Chapter

In this chapter we'll explore four ways we can reconnect our data to meaningful parts of education work: our values, our personal agency, our personal systems, and psychological safety.

Suggested Reflection

As you read this chapter, make the learning personal by answering these questions:

- ♦ When have you felt good about using data?
- ♦ During that time, what were you working on?
- ♦ What personal meaning did that activity have for you?

In the last chapter, we learned about the limitations of end-of-year test scores and other single measures of achievement to tell the full story of our students. But we can't ignore another important part of successful student experiences: us. Let's explore how

DOI: 10.4324/9781003139751-4

using data in practical ways helps us have the professional experiences we want for ourselves.

Connecting With Our Values

Let's begin this chapter with two stories that illustrate the connection between our values and how we use data in schools. As you read, reflect on how you would use data to serve your students if you were free to do so however you wanted.

When Values and Data Don't Connect

Cecilia (not her real name), works with data for a state department of education in the southern United States. Cecilia is professional, dedicated, and passionate about positive outcomes for students in and out of school. That was clear to me when I spoke to her for this book. For example, she shared her concern that the needs of students living in low-income neighborhoods were being overlooked. But ultimately, it was a story from Cecilia's past that really got my attention.

Cecilia shared a story that showed me what happens when school systems use data in a way that doesn't align with values. The story takes place a few years ago, before Cecilia worked for the state department of education. Back then, she was a data analyst in a school district. Cecilia's job was to work with student-level data. She analyzed that data and shared findings with decision makers.

Outside of work, Cecilia mentored a student who was homeless. The student was regularly suspended from school, and Cecilia became increasingly concerned that the suspensions were from behaviors stemming from the student's trauma.

Being a natural researcher, she started poring through district data. She researched how often students were suspended and the negative impact these suspensions had on their lives. She was concerned and alarmed by the findings: Cecilia's analysis showed that educators in her school district were suspending young students in minority racial groups at higher rates.[1]

Cecilia wrote a report of her findings and shared it with others in her district, hoping the findings would lead to more inquiry. Instead, district leaders were concerned about the political impact of the findings. While they shared the same concern about the unequal rates of suspension, their motivation to act did not rise to the same level as Cecilia's. They chose not to share the report with others. This was devastating to Cecilia. She eventually left the school district to take a job at a state department of education.

Cecilia experienced what I suspect many educators do: when we use data in a way that's disconnected to our personal and professional values, we feel discouraged.[2] We begin to feel that data is the *opposite* of practical—it has no functional connection to the positive and enriching school experience we want for our students. And when data stops feeling practical, we begin thinking of it only as something we're required to use instead of something that we want to use.

Fortunately, in my experience, the inverse is also true. Let's look at another story.

Moving the Analysis From Students to Adults

Patti Hershfeldt and Susan Barrett are part of a team that trains educators all over the United States. Their focus is on an intervention framework called Positive Behavioral Interventions and Supports (PBIS).[3] What struck me about their stories was how, in slightly different ways, their values shaped their ideas about practical data use early in their careers.

For Susan, there was something about the way school systems influenced individual behavior that nagged at her. She could observe individual student behaviors with her own eyes. What she couldn't see was how elements of the school system—instruction, norms, interventions, and measurements—influenced these individual behaviors.

Over time, Susan learned she could use data to get at that question: "We looked at student-level data, but we could step back and look at aggregate data like school climate surveys. And that painted a picture of how we can adapt the system to fit student strengths and needs rather than focusing on asking students to change."

Patti's story played out in a similar way, but with interesting differences. For Patti, it was the gap between educational research and everyday practice that nagged at her. She knew there was useful research being produced all the time but could not see how it was used in the classroom. The most important question to Patti was, how can we connect data with what actually happens in the classroom?

Patti recalled the moment when she realized the answer to this question. Early in her teaching career, Patti's supervisor sent her to a PBIS conference. At the conference, Patti spoke with George Sugai, now a senior advisor at the Center for PBIS. Patti shared how Sugai's talk inspired her to see data not only as a tool for improving student learning, but also as a tool to improve the educator's craft.

From that point forward, she thought about how data can help educators participate better in school systems. She described it to me this way: "[George Sugai] moved the unit of analysis away from students and put it on adults. This was an a-ha moment."

Susan's and Patti's stories are different in their details. But they're similar in this way: their use of data became practical the moment they chose to use it in response to the education issues that deeply mattered to them.

Data Can't Be Practical Without You

My elementary school basketball coach used to record our games and watch the videos afterward. He'd say things like, "Estrellado! You didn't follow the play." Then I'd stare at him blankly, because who can remember what they did in a basketball game they played a week ago? My coach responded with his version of the truth: "The video doesn't lie."

We hear this about data all the time: "The data doesn't lie." We're drawn to the allure of data in helping fields like education and healthcare—it makes us feel like we can work around the blind spots we can't see.

Except it's not that simple. It's true that data doesn't lie. But it's not because data takes a moral stand against lying. Data doesn't do anything on its own. *It's what we do with data that makes the difference.*

Consider this example: a genetics lab takes a person's DNA sample and analyzes it.[4] They report that the person has a 25 percent higher than average chance of diabetes. Can that number lie? No, because the number doesn't mean anything until the person uses it. And if that person uses it by incorrectly believing they have a 25 percent *chance* of the disease instead of a *higher than average* chance of the disease, they'd be wrong.

The idea that data doesn't lie isn't incorrect, it's just not complete. What's missing is the part people play in the equation. The data doesn't lie when we don't allow it to. And the data doesn't tell the truth unless we use it responsibly.

If that thought feels intimidating, consider this reframe: if we don't like the way we use data in our schools, we can change it. We can acknowledge our contribution to our organization's data culture and choose to do it differently. Let's look at two ways we can do that.

Connecting to Our Personal Systems

I've read that if you're seasick on a boat, it helps to take the helm.[5] There's something about steering the ship and putting your eyes on the horizon that stabilizes you. I don't know how true that is, but I like the imagery.

When you feel unsteady using data, respond by steering the boat and looking at the horizon. That means going beyond using data because it's a requirement. Instead, find ways to use data to support the daily planning, routines, and actions that contribute to the experience you want for your students.

One teacher, we'll call her Niki, shared how she organized her data collection based on her instructional focus:

> Especially when I teach US 2, there are a few units where there is no large summative assignment because it just doesn't fit with where I want the major focus of the course to be . . . . In all, we have 10 units and only 7 of them have some kind of project or major summative assessment.[6]

Niki also said this: "Most of my units have a particular skill attached to them, but others don't because we have content to plow through. I don't have major skills attached to the units I don't have major summative assessments for."

Look a little closer at Niki's approach and notice how she connects her data use to the goals she has for her students. Niki starts by saying:

> there are a few units where there is no large summative assignment because it just doesn't fit with where I want the major focus of the course to be.

Notice how Niki chooses when to give the summative assignments. She doesn't give them in areas that she's not focusing on. Instead, she starts by deciding the area of focus for her students. Then she assigns summative assessments where those areas of focus are.

Connect your data use to your values, personal agency, and personal systems and you'll find yourself inspired to use data more. But these individual decisions aren't the end of your journey. School systems are networks of individuals. And networks thrive when its members share learning with each other. For that to happen, you'll need psychological safety.

Psychological Safety and Sharing Data

Imagine the last time you went to a data meeting. What did it feel like when your teammates looked at data from your classroom,

school, or project? If it felt like submitting a drawing to be cri-
tiqued or playing the first note of a piano recital, you're not alone.

Sharing data from your classroom or school isn't just sharing
numbers. It's a way of sharing the product of your hard work. And
if you're like me, sharing your work feels vulnerable. It's taking an
object you put your heart and soul into—like a painting, an essay,
or a meal—and putting it in front of everyone. It's a vulnerable act.

When sharing doesn't feel safe, sharing won't lead to learning. That's because feedback and collaboration get hijacked by
all kinds of emotions—shame, defensiveness, fear, and others.
In her book *Daring Greatly*, Brené Brown writes about "armoring
up" ahead of feedback.[7] It's what we do when we're afraid of
putting our work out there.

Here's more from Brené Brown:, "Armored feedback doesn't
facilitate lasting and meaningful change—I don't know a single person who can be open to accepting feedback or owning
responsibility for something when they're being hammered. Our
hardwiring takes over and we self-protect." Ah, yes. Yet another
example of how practical data use is not so different from our
other professional duties.

At your next data meeting, try this: share some data from your
classroom or school. It should be something slightly uncomfort-
able, but nothing that sends you down a spiral of emotions. Then
invite your peers to comment on it using a question like this:

> I noticed the average score on this last round of assess-
> ments was lower than the past three. I'm concerned about
> that, but I'm not sure what's happening there. What
> would your next steps be if you were me? Any sugges-
> tions for how else I can work with this?

I use questions like this for three reasons: first, it starts with my
concerns about what I'm seeing in the data. Second, it's a friendly
invitation to participate in my process. And third, it's a subtle
signal that I trust my peers with my work, and they can trust
me with theirs.

Back to Brené Brown, who does a much better job than me of explaining why this approach is useful: "The simple and honest process of letting people know that discomfort is normal, it's going to happen, why it happens, and why it's important, reduces anxiety, fear, and shame."

Here's a bonus tip for administrators: model how to share data in a way that invites feedback and maintains safety in your data culture. Your staff looks to you to set the expectations. So if you want data to be used more frequently and practically in your organization, get vulnerable and show them how it's done. They'll appreciate you for it.[8]

I believe that being an educator is a creative job. Teachers create experiences for their students. Principals create experiences for their staff. And like other creative professionals, sharing their work—data-related or otherwise—is how we serve people and improve our craft. Make it safe to do that more often, and you'll be on your way to a healthier data culture.

Conclusion

Expanding our concept of school data beyond test scores is not only good for students, it's good for educators. When we reimagine data use as a way to access the parts of our craft we're passionate about, data becomes a motivating tool instead of a chore.[9]

Data use can help us express our values or it can stifle them. It can inspire collaboration in safe environments or can hinder it in punishing ones. It's up to us which story about data we want to believe.

Activity: Making Your Data Meetings Safe

What This Does

In this activity, you'll learn how to create data meeting norms that encourage safety and creativity.

How This Can Help Us

School data is a representation of our work, so sharing it is a vulnerable act. Our meeting norms should help us learn about what's working for our students, share successful techniques, and share stories. When we reduce fear and increase trust, we have more sharing and critical thinking. And when that happens, we build a safe environment where we learn together about what we can do today to support our students better.

Follow These Steps

Imagine your ideal conversations: Describe the conversations that will lead to collective learning and benefit for your students. Try these sentence frames:

- ◆ "When we talk about data, I want to learn more about _____."
- ◆ "When we talk about data, I don't want to feel worried that _____."
- ◆ "I make the best decisions for my students when _____."

Identify productive behaviors: Describe behaviors that result in the kind of data conversations you want. Consider these examples:

- ◆ A week before each meeting, our team begins to gather information to bring and discuss.
- ◆ When someone needs help gathering or understanding data, we meet them where they are and learn together.
- ◆ When tense situations arise, we avoid blaming someone and focus on how our team is positioned to improve.

Post in a visible place: Capture these behaviors in a list that's visible during your data meetings. These will evolve over time, so it's worthwhile to start with just a few. No more than five norms is a good place to start.

Review and improve: Pick a date on the calendar to review the norms. During this review, ask questions like: "How well are these norms making it safe to share and discuss data for decision-making?"

Notes

1. For more on inequality in discipline events, see Skiba et al. "Parsing Disciplinary Disproportionality: Contributions of Infraction, Student, and School Characteristics to Out-of-School Suspension and Expulsion," *American Education Research Journal*, 2014.
2. There's been some research about the relationship between personal values and ethical behavior in the workplace. Damodar, Suar, and Rooplekha Khuntia. "Influence of Personal Values and Value Congruence on Unethical Practices and Work Behavior." *Journal of Business Ethics*, 2010.
3. For more about PBIS, see California PBIS Coalition. "What is PBIS?" California PBIS Coalition, https://pbisca.org/what-is-pbis%3F. Accessed 30 April 2021.
4. I found this example in Rosenblat, Alex, et al. "Interpretation Gone Wrong." *The Social, Cultural & Ethical Dimensions of "Big Data,"* 2014.
5. Boater, Dan. "17 Easy Ways to Beat Seasickness Right Now." *Dan Boater*, https://danboater.org/travel-health-and-safety/17-easy-ways-to-beat-seasickness-right-now.html. Accessed 30 April 2021.
6. I lightly edited this quote and used a false name to make it easier to read. NoSpice4Me. "What does assessment look like in your classroom." *Reddit*, www.reddit.com/r/Teachers/comments/azj56u/what_does_assessment_look_like_in_your_classroom/. Accessed 30 April 2021.
7. Brown, Brené. *Daring Greatly: How the Courage to Be Vulnerable Transforms the Way We Live, Love, Parent, and Lead*. Avery, 2015.
8. Meyer, Frauk, et al. "How Leaders Communicate Their Vulnerability: Implications for Trust Building." *International Journal of Educational Management*, vol. 31, 2017, pp. 221–235.
9. Kim, Inyoung, and William E. Loadman. "Psychological Conditions of Personal Engagement and Disengagement at Work." Academy of Management Journal, 1990, pp. 692–724.

4

Time Is the Problem

In This Chapter

In this chapter we'll explore challenges and solutions for learning to use data on the job.

Suggested Reflection

As you read this chapter, make the learning personal by answering these questions:

- ♦ Where are the small opportunities in your day where you can practice the techniques from this book?
- ♦ How will you remind yourself that a little learning regularly is more impactful than a lot of learning every once in a while?
- ♦ How will you know you've added too much data work to your routine? How will you know you need to add more?

DOI: 10.4324/9781003139751-5

In 2001, I was training to be a school psychologist. During the day, I worked as an intern at a middle school in southern California. Then, after work, I drove an hour south to San Diego State University. I sat in the food court eating middle-of-the-road Chinese food while writing reports until my evening classes started.

That fall, the topic of evening classes was a noble one: learn to write reports using every possible best practice of school psychology. As a result, I spent weeks writing a single report. At the end of the course, I turned the report in. It was over twenty pages long.

One year later, I got my first real job in public education and faced a professional tension I still grapple with today. On my first day as a school psychologist in the largest elementary school district in California, I sat in my office in front of a long list of students I needed to work with. The thought of writing the perfect report for each of these students seemed at once the correct thing to do and also impossible.

Something interesting happens after we graduate from our training programs and start our education careers. We learn that the idealized version of our craft, as imagined in graduate school courses, doesn't fit perfectly into the reality of working in schools.

If you're a teacher, the workaday lesson plans aren't as detailed as the ones you made in graduate school. If you're a school counselor, you work on student schedules more and run counseling groups less. If you're a principal, you spend more time working on administrative tasks and less time executing your school's instructional vision.[1]

To develop a meaningful data practice, we need to address the rarest of resources: time.[2]

Use Small Learning Moments Often

In a moment, I'll share some ideas for breaking up your data practice into practical parts so you can learn throughout the day and build your data skill over time. But first, let's take a short break from data and look at a related example: how I write books while working a full-time education job.

Here's what a typical day looks like for me: I get up while it's still dark. I go downstairs and start the coffee. As the sound of percolating wake-up juice fills the kitchen, I head out for a walk with my writing partner, a pug named Marcy.

When we get back to the house, I feed Marcy breakfast. I pour my coffee. Marcy finishes the meal in under five minutes and retreats to the couch to nap for the rest of the morning. I sit down at the kitchen table, take a deep focusing breath, and sit down to write.

After around forty-five minutes of writing, I get ready for work, then hop in the car with my son. We drive and talk and listen to music. Then I drop him off at the nearby middle school.

After I drop my son off, I drive to work. My son's first bell is really early, so I arrive at work before anyone else. I get out of the driver's seat and hop into the passenger's seat. I get my laptop out and write for another twenty minutes in the stark quiet of an empty parking lot.

At 8:00, the workday starts. At work, I look for small opportunities to practice my writing. And I mean small: emails, memos, presentation slides, and notes to myself. Take emails, for example: before I hit send, I reflect for a few seconds. Is this easy for my coworker to read? Are there words and sentences I can cut to make it even easier?

There are many small moments in the day we can use to practice. When I use these small moments to learn, I get consistent training. I've had many versions of this routine throughout my life. It wasn't always about writing. At one point I was learning photography. During another I was learning about data science. And in yet another I was learning to exercise more.

Looking back, I see the problem was not an absence of time. It was that the amount of available time was so miniscule that it seemed inconsequential.

*****

When we do something consistently, even if only a little at a time, we get better at it. It feels slow and pointless at first, but trust me on this: using small opportunities to learn often creates the conditions for your skill to develop. It won't happen immediately, but eventually we realize we're operating on a different level than before.

Keeping the learning moments small and frequent will empower you to use them consistently.[3] When are the small moments in your day that you can collect data? When are the small moments in your day that you can look at data? What are other data activities you can try regularly, if given a few minutes?

These small moments will be different for everyone, but use these examples to start a brainstorm about your version of this:

◆ Pick a small data collection method that you can use every day. Pick one that's both quick and meaningful. Here's an example I like: I read a story where a teacher suggested timing transitions from one activity to the next.[4] It's quick—it probably takes a minute or less. And it's meaningful—it helps the teacher improve the transition routine.

◆ Schedule time in your calendar for regular data work: I have a calendar event for myself every Friday to download data from our special education data system. That dataset goes into a folder with previous weeks so I can analyze it later.

◆ Review a cumulative file for a student in your classroom. Once you've reviewed ten of these, start looking for themes across cumulative files. How often do students change schools? What neighborhoods do your students live in? These can be inspiration for new things to try in the classroom.

How to Organize Your Learning Moments

Now that you've shrunk your data activities to bite size daily pieces, let's find moments in the day where you can do them.

Try organizing your moments in Table 4.1. When you get these moments out of your head and onto the page, you can look, think, and plan your routines.

In the first column, name the activity. In the second column, write down how long the activity takes. In the third column, write a time of day when you could work on this consistently. Here's an example:

TABLE 4.1 Organize Your Learning Moments

Activity	Estimated Time	When Can I Do This
Organize your qualitative data by highlighting stories and interesting observations in your notebook.	10 min	During student independent work on Thursdays
Enter exit slip scores into a spreadsheet.	30 min	During prep
Review spreadsheets.	5 min	During student independent work on Wednesdays
Brainstorm things to change based on the spreadsheet.	10 min	During prep
Share data with a teammate.	15 min	During the break at the weekly staff meeting
Brainstorm new lesson ideas to try and how you'd know if they worked.	15 min	Right after dismissal

This table is a brainstorming tool, not a schedule. The goal of the exercise is not to pack your whole day with data activities. That's not sustainable—you'll burn out fast. Instead, pick one or two you can commit to. Fit the rest in when you can. If you pick something meaningful that you can do regularly, your data skill will snowball over time. And you'll start organically branching out to other new and exciting ways to use data practically.

Use Existing Routines

What if the idea of adding anything extra to your already full schedule stresses you out? I know the feeling. Try starting with a smaller step.

Rather than add another routine to your day that's already filled with routines, try picking one and finding a way to use it for data practice. This works because you're latching on to a routine you're already accustomed to using. You're not adding brand new activities to your day. You're just adjusting the ones that are already there.

Let's say you have a ten-minute chunk of prep time that looks like this (Table 4.2):

TABLE 4.2 Prep Time

	Monday	Tuesday	Wednesday	Thursday	Friday
8:20–8:30	Prep: Grading	Prep: Planning	Prep: Grading	Prep: Planning	Prep: General

Instead of finding a new time slot in the day to do your data work, try folding it into your existing routine.[5] In this example, I've added related data activities—data entry, reviewing exit slips, and organizing small groups based on those exit slips (Table 4.3):

TABLE 4.3 Prep Time With Data Activities

	Monday	Tuesday	Wednesday	Thursday	Friday
8:20–8:30	Prep: Grading + Data Entry	Prep: Planning + Review Exit Slips	Prep: Grading + Data Entry	Prep: Planning + Organize Small Groups	Prep: General

The key word here is "related." When your data use directly supports what you're trying to accomplish with your time, you've made it practical. For example, if Monday is the day that you grade quizzes and projects, you can also use that time to enter the grades into a spreadsheet. All the activities connect to the larger goal: understand what your students have learned and plan your next steps.

And on top of that, you're not asking your brain to adjust to a new schedule. You're just using your current schedule as a trigger for a new behavior.

Your routine is the secret weapon. Learn on the job. Prioritize consistency over perfection. Shrink the actions down to something small enough that they're repeatable. Trust that if you do a little every day, you'll build skill over time in meaningful ways. And most importantly, you'll build it in a way that is practical for you.

Balance Your Digital and Non-Digital Tools[6]

By now, you've broken your data tasks down to small learning moments. You've analyzed your daily routines and found regular opportunities to experience these learning moments. Now let's talk about how to get the most out of your daily data use.

To do that, you'll need rapid cycles that go back and forth between trial and error, revision, and trying again.[7] Some sources of data will help you do that better than others. To find those, start thinking of your data sources as two categories: the ones you control and the ones you don't.

Let's start with that first category. Data sources you control are the ones you generate throughout the regular course of your work. Many times these data sources are analog, but not always. Some examples of data sources you make are observation notes, quiz scores, exit tickets,[8] and behavior tracking sheets. You made the form, you entered the data, and you analyzed the results. Student cumulative files also fall in this category because they're analog and in some cases you can change how they're organized to suit your data use better.

And now the second category: data sources you don't control. These are data that someone else controls. Most of the time these data sources are digital, but not always. Some examples are online assessments, student attendance systems, literacy software, and online behavior trackers.

Here's a rule of thumb: spend more time with the first category while you figure out what you need from your data. Once you know more about how you want to use the data to make decisions, start spending more and more time with the second category.

A great way to get value from the limited time you have is to start by investing in your self-awareness about what data is meaningful to you. Then, when you start using more and more third-party data tools, you'll have a discerning eye for what's useful to you and what's not. Spending time with data sources you control helps because you can make adjustments to your system as you learn what you need (Figure 4.1).

Finding a System That Works

	High Control	Low Control
Small scale	Exit slips Behavior trackers Quiz scores Cumulative files	(Spend the least time with these)
Large scale	(The unicorn of data. Hard to find in schools)	Online assessments Student record systems Public enrollment data

Learn what works for you with these

Then take what you learned and reach the most students with these

FIGURE 4.1 Start by experimenting with sources of data you control. Once you learn how data supports your daily decisions, start looking for larger scale data systems like the ones you find in student databases and literacy software. Avoid data you can't control and also doesn't offer you scale. Those are the worst of both worlds.

For example, do you find it useful to organize small groups by sorting exit slip scores? You can create a spreadsheet with three columns: name, date of exit slip, and score. And importantly, now you're aware of the kind of data you need to make the decisions that matter to you. As you bring third party data tools into your daily routine, you now have enough awareness to ask questions like "Does this data tool help me organize my small groups faster and more accurately than my exit slip scores?"

Keeping Overhead Low

I want to close this chapter with a story about a teacher, Megan, who organizes her resources to make the best use of her time. When I spoke to Megan in the fall of 2020, she was teaching at an elementary school in Seattle, Washington. To get warmed up for our interview, I asked Megan which resources she'd been using in her work. I could tell this was an exciting topic for her because she immediately went off camera (it was a virtual call) and looked through her books.

She came back with a book about math instruction called *Number Talks*, by Sherry Parrish.[9] "It's a strategy for teaching math. The sections are fun and short. I know I can get something out of this book, so I reference this one a lot."

What Megan liked most about this book is how quickly she could start experimenting with the ideas. "It's fun because I feel like I can just flip through it. It's simple but it's powerful. There's not a lot of overhead to try something like this."

Overhead. That word stuck with me. It's a word usually used to describe the cost of doing business. I hadn't heard it used in the context of reading a book. I asked Megan to tell me more:

I had the book but then getting started felt overwhelming. I needed to pick an activity and try it. And if I couldn't do it perfectly the first time, that was ok. I knew I could read it and get started with something in 5 minutes.

When we're building up a skill, we need to find time to do it regularly. But sometimes time isn't the only barrier. We can also get so overwhelmed that we don't get started. We can all learn something from Megan's advice: it won't be perfect and we won't learn it all at once. But if we try something small every day, we'll improve.

This is also true for learning to use data on the job. So much of it hinges on just getting started with some regularity. How do we get ourselves unstuck so we can just start? Megan shared more about her methods.

First, she focuses on ideas she can try right away. That way, she can just try the idea without worrying about how long it'll take to get set up. Megan describes this approach as "keeping overhead low."

Second, she doesn't expect perfection from herself. She knows getting started is more important than getting it perfect. That's because she can always improve and make adjustments along the way.

And finally, Megan finds new activities that are fun. She knows she feels joy when she's doing the work, not thinking about doing the work. And so she gravitates towards activities that empower her to try fun things with her students right away.

Megan's approach works because she's acting on her own internal resources, which ultimately she controls. She chooses the types of activities she does. She chooses to value getting started over getting it perfect.

The same applies to how you can learn to use data meaningfully throughout your busy workday. I've included many practical data activities in this book (check at the end of each chapter and also in the appendix). Find one you can start in a few minutes. Find one that sounds fun. And just get started, even if it feels clunky at first. Rinse and repeat, and over time, almost imperceptibly, you'll begin using data more and more practically.

Conclusion

In this chapter, we reimagined practical data use by reframing one of the most practical challenges of all: there are more tasks to do than there are hours to do them. We explored ideas for small changes that have long-term impact. And we explored keeping our learning overhead low by picking ideas we can start right away. Afterall, time won't change for us. The next best thing is to adapt our learning to the time we have.

The routines you build and evolve to address this problem will be personal to you. Once you have your routine dialed in, it's time to start identifying data you'll see in the field. In the next section, I'll be introducing a guide to commonly seen data in schools for you to reference as you execute your practical data use.

Activity: Organize, Learn, and Scale

There's no getting around it: learning what practical data use means for you takes time. But why take more time than you need to? Here's how to organize your data, learn on the job, and reach the most students, all in one workflow.

What This Does

In this activity, you'll set up a workflow to organize data, learn what data works best for you, and find new data sources to reach even more students.

How This Can Help Us

Educators have a lot of data they could use. Through trial and error, they've got to learn which data serves their daily decision-making. And once they've learned that, they've got to keep that data coming efficiently so they can reach even more students.

This activity connects three steps together in a chain: organize your data sources, use trial and error to learn what helps you the most, and scale with more data sources.

This will reduce the time it takes you to find the most practical data. And it will help you act on it intentionally instead of feeling overwhelmed.

Instructions

1. Make a list of the data sources available to you. Think broadly. Some examples are quiz scores, observation notes, state testing results, and reports from instructional software.

2. Sort these data sources into two columns: in column A, list the data sources that you make and can improve on the job. This is where you'd include data sources like cumulative files, which you generally have control over even if you don't create all the data. In column B, list the data sources that someone else (usually a software company or education agency) makes for you (Table 4.4).

3. For two weeks, spend the majority of your data work experimenting with the sources in column A. Revise how you use them until they reflect a strong connection between the data and your most important decisions.

4. Once you can verbalize how you use the data sources in column A, look to column B for more efficient ways of getting similar data. Try this sentence frame: *My favorite way to use data in column A is _____. I can try making that more efficient by experimenting with _____ in column B.*

TABLE 4.4 Example: List of Data Sources

Column A: Data You Make	Column B: Data Someone Else Makes
Exit slips	Online assessments
Behavior trackers	Student record systems
Quiz scores	Public enrollment data
Cumulative files	

Example: The Thought Process

I can enter exit slip results into a spreadsheet, then sort it to organize small groups for next week. Once I run the groups, I can use another round of exit slips to see how well the plan worked.

Two weeks later . . .

I learned the exit slip data helped when I could sort the scores in a spreadsheet. The classroom software we use has a lot of reports. I wonder if I can sort scores, not only from last week's assessment on expressions but also the one on ratios before that? There might be more opportunities to reteach.

Notes

1. Horng, Eileen L., et al. "Principal Time-Use and School Effectiveness." Calder Urban Institute, 2009, www.urban.org/sites/default/files/publication/28151/1001441-Principal-Time-Use-and-School-Effectiveness.PDF. Accessed 4 June 2021.
2. Data Quality Campaign. "Teachers See the Power of Data But Don't Have Enough Time to Use It." Data Quality Campaign, 12 September 2018, https://dataqualitycampaign.org/resource/teachers-see-the-power-of-data-but-dont-have-enough-time-to-use-it/. Accessed 2 June 2021.
3. This idea is explored in books like Clear, James. Atomic Habits: An Easy & Proven Way to Build Good Habits & Break Bad Ones. Avery, 2018 and Maurer, Robert. One Small Step Can Change Your Life: The Kaizen Way. Workman Publishing Company, 2014.
4. Bielefeld, Lelly. "Improving Classroom Routines With Data." Mimio Educator, 20 June 2017, https://blog.mimio.com/improving-classroom-routines-with-data. Accessed 2 June 2021.
5. Again, from James Clear's Atomic Habits. This is an idea he calls "habit stacking." Clear, James. Atomic Habits: An Easy & Proven Way to Build Good Habits & Break Bad Ones. Avery, 2018.
6. I found this terminology in a paper by the Bill and Melinda Gates Foundation. Bill and Melinda Gates Foundation. "Teachers Know

Best: Making Data Work for Teachers and Students." 2021. Bill and Melinda Gates Foundation, https://s3.amazonaws.com/edtech-production/reports/Gates-TeachersKnowBest-MakingDataWork.pdf. Accessed 22 May 2021.
7. For more on this idea, see the chapter about Plan Do Study Act cycles in Bryk, Anthony S., et al. Learning to Improve: How America's Schools Can Get Better at Getting Better. Harvard Education Publishing, 2015.
8. For more on creating and using exit tickets as a quick assessment, see Edutopia. "Gaining Understanding on What Your Students Know." Edutopia, 23 June 2015, www.edutopia.org/practice/exit-tickets-checking-understanding. Accessed 29 August 2021.
9. The book that Megan showed me was Parrish, Sherry. Number Talks: Whole Number Computation. Math Solutions, 2014.

Part 2
Your Data Field Guide

One day, I was having coffee with my dear friend Sean in his backyard on a sunny weekend morning. He had recently gotten into bird watching, a subject I knew nothing about. So I asked him about how it works.

When Sean sees a bird or hears a bird making sounds, he takes notes in a notebook or on his phone. What color was the bird? How big was it? What sound did it make? Then, later, Sean consults a bird guidebook to match his observations to the bird watching community's volume of knowledge. From this comparison, Sean makes the best guess at what bird he saw and, in the process, expands his vocabulary and general knowledge of these wondrous flying creatures.

When we learn about something new, like practical data use in schools, it helps to have a go-to reference—a sort of field guide for data use. We start by learning to identify new data sources we see. Then we learn how to name these new wondrous things, and in doing so we learn to talk about them. Then, as our experience deepens, we learn the nuances of these data sources, both their usefulness and their limitations.

I can't promise that you'll see brightly colored birds on the job, but I'm near certain you'll be asked to work with data. And as you learn to work with data, I hope this section helps you do that meaningfully and practically.

Read this if:

♦ You want to learn how to identify commonly seen sources of data in schools and school districts

DOI: 10.4324/9781003139751-6

- You want to learn the upsides and downsides of each of these data sources
- You want to learn new vocabulary so you can talk about data confidently and share information with others
- You're looking for a reference to keep on your office shelf as a go-to guide for working with school data

Activities In This Section

You'll find these activities at the end of each chapter in this section:

1. Parts of Charts.
2. Making Your Own Tables.
3. Student-Level Data Organizer.
4. Turning Accountability Data Into Local Data.

5

Charts

In This Chapter

In this chapter, you'll learn about

- ♦ How to identify different kinds of data charts
- ♦ Examples of charts you'll see at work
- ♦ A routine for using charts
- ♦ How to talk about charts

Suggested Reflection

As you read this chapter, make the learning personal by answering these questions:

- ♦ What kind of charts do you see in your daily work?
- ♦ Which charts do you see the most?
- ♦ What would it look like, sound like, and feel like if you could explain that chart to a teammate?

DOI: 10.4324/9781003139751-7

Fifteen minutes into one of Dr. Stephanie Evergreen's talks about data visualization, attendees realize there's something different about it. Evergreen, Founder of Evergreen Data, is clearly an expert—people know that when they sign up. But her approach is so accessible they almost forget they're at a data training. Her style is scientific, human, and oriented towards social justice.

I recently attended one of her talks, in which she opened with the Beatles' *Here Comes the Sun*, then showed off her Beatles t-shirt. Casual pleasantries out of the way, she began teaching data visualization lessons from her deep base of research. But in Evergreen fashion, she discussed relatable artifacts, including roadside signage, presentation slide pie charts, and news articles.

Evergreen began her career by studying early childhood education in college. After that, she started teaching. Eventually her path led her to a doctoral program in interdisciplinary research where she studied, among other things, statistics, sociology, public health, and education.

If you've ever wondered how an expert in interdisciplinary research works, Evergreen's story provides the answer. As a PhD student, she spent her days designing, conducting, analyzing, and writing about survey data. It was this work that would lead her to an important lesson and eventually to her career as a data visualization expert.

While researching, she noticed a problem: she was creating important new knowledge to help educators, but few in the field were using it to improve their craft.

She needed to try something different: "That's when I started thinking about the visual aspect of data . . . . And I desperately needed a dissertation topic. So I chose to become an expert in data visualization." Shortly after, she saw signs that her new approach was sparking interest. One of those signs came at a

2009 conference, where she would see for herself how much data visualization spoke to people.

As Evergreen mentally prepared to take the stage for her talk, she didn't know what to expect. Stephanie stepped into the hall and was surprised to see three hundred people waiting for her: "I wasn't expecting it. There were so many people crowded up at the front I could barely move around." The crowd at her talk, and at the many talks that followed, spoke to the importance of data visualization as a practical data tool.

Sometimes they're called visualizations. Other times they're called plots. And still other times they're called charts. For our purposes, we'll use these terms interchangeably. The important thing is to get you on the path to interpreting and sharing them confidently.

How to Spot Charts

If learning about data was *actually* like bird watching, charts would be the morning doves and blue jays of the education data world. You see them all the time.

We can find them in reports that come out of the software our students use. We can find them on websites that display school data like enrollment figures and test scores. And we can find them in research papers. They are some of the most available sources of data, so learning to use them well is a good investment in time. As you look at some of these examples, see if you recognize any from your workday.

Examples of Charts

Bar Charts: Bar charts help you compare quantities in two or more categories. Each bar represents a quantity. Bar charts are effective because the brain is good at comparing lengths of things, as long as those things have a common baseline.

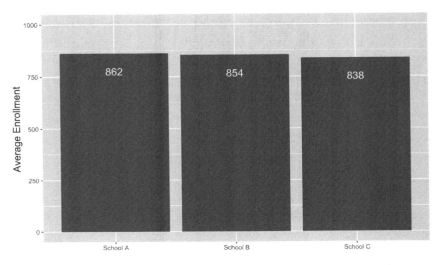

FIGURE 5.1 Average Enrollment from 2015–2019. Bar charts help us because our brains are good at comparing lengths if the bars have a common baseline.

Here's what I mean by that: imagine a parent and a child standing next to each other, where the child is exactly half the height of the parent. It will be easy to guess the difference in height. Now imagine the child is standing on a step stool, thus creating two different baselines. You'll still see that there is a height difference, but you'll find it harder to estimate how big that difference is.

Stacked Bar Charts: Then there's the close relative to the bar chart, the stacked bar chart. This visualization helps you compare quantities across bars and within each bar. Stacked bar charts are useful because you can make multiple comparisons. Just be careful about your estimates of length within each bar. They don't have a common baseline, so you'll find it harder to make accurate comparisons.

Pie Chart: This is a pie chart. It helps us compare the size of each part within a whole. Each "slice" of the pie is a quantity making up the whole "pie." They can help you when differences between slices are big enough to be obvious. But they are

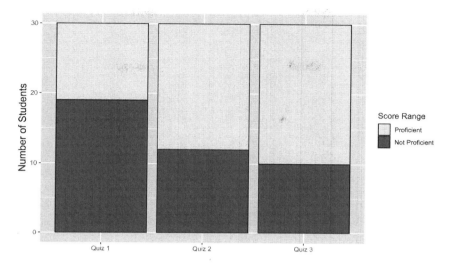

FIGURE 5.2 Score Ranges by Quiz. Each quiz was taken by 30 students. Stacked bar charts help us compare quantities across bars and within bars. But be careful with your estimates. Only the bottom stack of each bar has a common baseline with the other bars.

notoriously difficult to estimate when there are too many slices or the slices are small.[1]

In contrast to how the brain compares lengths of bars with a common baseline, the brain struggles to compare the angles at the narrow end of the pie slices. When you estimate differences between pie slices, use caution and try to look at other sources of data too.

By now you're putting a name to the charts you see in your everyday work. The dots are connecting and you now know what to call these charts when you see them. Let's explore how they can help us.

What Charts Are Useful For

Charts are popular data tools for a reason: they help us get more out of our brain power, which generally taps out once there's too much data to make sense of.

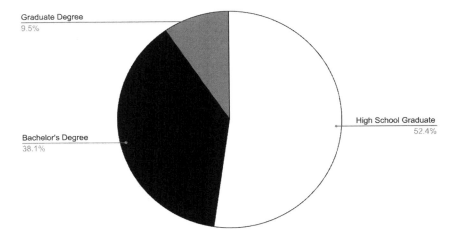

FIGURE 5.3 Educational Attainment. Pie charts help us give a rough sense of proportion. Look for ones that have larger "slices." The smaller the slices, the harder it is to compare them to each other. For example, it's hard to estimate how much smaller the slice for "Graduate Degree" is compared to the slice for "High School Graduate".

That's because charts help us use our brains to detect patterns.[2] When done well, they use visual features to give our short-term memory an assist. Instead of struggling to remember numbers and detect patterns at the same time, charts use visual elements like color, size, and length to communicate information.[3] Our brains respond to these visual features almost instantaneously.

How do you use this super tool in your everyday work? Lots of ways, but here's one you might have missed: you can use charts to prepare for data meetings. In the days leading up to a meeting, start noting when you see useful charts of student data like quiz scores, attendance, or assessments. Gather them up in a place where you can look at them during the meeting. These charts represent lots of data in a concise visual message, so use them as a reference as you listen and contribute to conversations at the meeting.

Here's another: you can use charts as a way to start conversations with students. In Amanda Datnow and Vicki Park's book *Data-Driven Leadership*, they described teachers doing just that. They used charts made from student work or assessments as conversation starters with students.[4] In doing so, they seized an opportunity to talk with their students about what they needed.

If it's not already obvious, charts are pretty great. But I find that the more nuance I bring to my data use, the more practical it is. And nothing brings out nuance like a good old pros and cons list.

We know the pros of charts. Now let's turn to their limitations.

Limitations of Charts

Our brains are amazing machines for instantaneously processing visuals and detecting patterns. But this is only a superpower when the visualizations are well designed.

For example, our brains are great at comparing lengths of visual elements. That's why bar charts are an effective tool for comparing data like test scores across different quizzes. But our brains aren't as good at comparing the sizes of shapes or angles. That's why pie charts are usually a poor choice for comparing quantities, especially when we've got a pie with too many slices.

In a perfect world, we'd have the best visualizations possible, based on the principles of good data science and visual design. In reality, the quality of data visualizations available to us is mixed. So how do we deal with that?

Practice being aware of charts where you're likely to make accurate interpretations and also ones where you're likely to make errors of interpretation. In cases of the latter, apply skepticism and explore other data sources before drawing conclusions. For example, since you know that people are more likely to estimate quantities accurately using bar charts than they are pie charts, think twice before making a decision on a single viewing of a multi-sliced pie. If the pie's all you've got, surround it with context, conversation, and debate.

Identifying Basic Chart Elements

There are countless variations of charts—certainly too many to cover here. But if you can learn to talk about a chart's basic visual elements, you'll have what you need to interpret and discuss the majority of charts you'll encounter in your classrooms and district office. These three elements are:

x-axis: The x-axis is the horizontal line that usually represents numbers or categories. In some cases, like in scatter plots, the x-axis can represent a range of numbers.[5]

y-axis: The y-axis is the vertical line that usually represents a range of numbers. The numbers can take different forms, like percentages. In some cases, like in bar charts that have been flipped so the bars are horizontal instead of vertical, the y-axis represents variables like schools or grade levels.

Visual elements that represent data points: These are the shapes on the grid of the plot that represent values, usually quantities. This is what you usually think of when you imagine charts: they're the bars, dots, and colors that help us use the data to make comparisons.

For example, have another look at the chart in Figure 5.1, "Average Enrollment Over the Last Five Years." In this chart, the x-axis represents the schools, the y-axis represents the average enrollment, and the height of each bar allows you to compare the average enrollment of each school.

Using Reasoning Questions

Now that you've got vocabulary for the chart's elements, you can reason with the data presented in the chart. Start by asking questions about what the chart's elements tell you.

Question the chart using this format:

What does the [VISUAL ELEMENT] tell us about the [X-AXIS] and the [Y-AXIS]?

Here's an example using a bar chart of formative assessment results by grade level. First the chart:

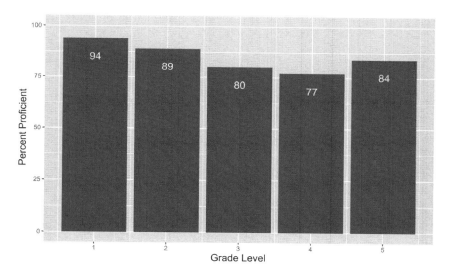

FIGURE 5.4 Percent of Students Who Scored in the Proficient Range. Formative assessment data from first through fifth graders.

. . . and now the question:

*What does the **length of each bar (visual element)** tell us about the **number (y-axis) of students in each grade level (x-axis)** who scored in the proficient range? A longer bar suggests a higher percentage of students who scored in the proficient range.*

Let's try another. Here's an example using a line chart. Line charts are useful for displaying changes in quantities over time. This example shows total enrollment at a school over time.

First the chart:

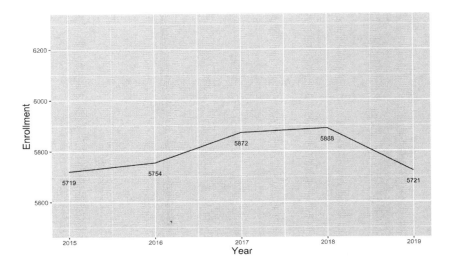

FIGURE 5.5 Enrollment Over Time. The last five years of enrollment data.

> . . . and now the question: *What does the **height (y-axis)** of each **dot (visual element)** tell us about the growth of total enrollment in the **last five years (x-axis)**? The height of the line tells us about the number of students enrolled in our school district. We can compare the height of the line at different dates to see how enrollment has changed.*

After doing this a few times, you'll start coming up with your own meaningful questions. Your professional intuition will guide you to the questions you need to ask so this process is useful for your everyday work. When you find the right questions, jot them down in a data notebook so you can use them with other charts.

Equity in Education

We can use charts to look at outcomes of student groups that school systems have historically underserved.[6] We can also use charts to learn about student groups in our local communities that aren't receiving the same benefit from our school system as others. Think broadly here: racial identity, gender identity, income level, living conditions, and disability.

Once you've built up some self-awareness about what you need from charts, apply it to finding the charts that help you explore equitable outcomes. Learn to notice and discuss when charts reveal or obscure inequality in schools.

Let's look at some ways to use charts as we work towards equitable results for our students.

Find Charts That Show Student Groups

First, look for charts that show data by student groups. You'll know you've found one because one of the axes will represent a student group. Here are some examples of charts that show data by student (or staff) group:

◆ Attendance by free and reduced lunch status
◆ Special education identification by racial groups
◆ Staff hiring by gender identity

When you pick charts that show student groups, you access stories that are harder to get to with charts that don't show student groups.

Don't Stop There. Take Action

Second, find ways to go from the chart to change in your daily work. Charts are a useful conversation starter because they help you find patterns across many data points. But that's only the start. Charts can and should be used to drive action.

For example, teachers at one school identified student groups they felt had little voice in the classroom.[7] They committed to learn more about three students each, then reflected on how the individual circumstances of these students affected their school experience.

That's how you go from data to action: start by looking at a few charts. Then ask yourself "What was this like from the point of view of a student? How can I find out?" Zoom in to the student level to appreciate the individual student stories. Go from aggregated data to disaggregated data. Go from general experiences to individual experiences. Go from your assumptions about your students to an individual student's story.

Use People First Language, Even If the Chart Doesn't

Finding students who don't have a voice and then honoring their value by connecting with them is something you can *do*. How about something you can *say*?

In their piece about racial equity awareness in data visualization, Jonathan Schwabish and Alice Feng urged data visualization creators to use humanizing language.[8] Their advice? Write and talk about people, not categories. Discuss students living in poverty instead of "poor students." Discuss the Asian student population instead of "Asians." Discuss students identified with a learning disability instead of "disabled students."

Unless you're creating the data visualization yourself, you can't control how chart titles, axis titles, and captions are written.[9] But you can and should choose to frame your discussions about charts by focusing on the people you serve, not the names of categories charts use to represent them.

The next time you and your colleagues look at a chart together, choose your words so you talk about people. You'll be well on your way to using charts with nuance and empathy.

Conclusion

In this chapter, you learned how to navigate charts with confidence by identifying the chart's elements. Armed with this new skill, you can continue practicing:

- ◆ Understanding how the elements of the chart represent its underlying data

♦ Thinking about how the chart reflects the experiences of your students

♦ Knowing when charts help us reason with the data, but also when they make us prone to errors in judgement and perception

For most of us, working with charts involves using them and not creating them. That puts us at the mercy of a chart's design.

But with your new skills and this chapter as an everyday reference, you can think critically about charts. This will help you use thoughtfully designed visualizations. Perhaps more importantly, it will help you get something out of less thoughtfully designed ones. And that will make your data use more practical.

In the next chapter, we'll turn our attention to the next subject of the data field guide. This one is also a data visual, but organized in a much different way.

Activity: Parts of Charts

If you're reading this book, charts might be the main way you consume data in your education job. This activity helps you identify practical uses for charts and pair them with questions to improve your interpretation.

What This Activity Does
This activity will help you practice some basic fact finding for charts.

How This Helps Us
Each data visualization is made up of different parts. The most complex data visualizations use several visual elements to communicate a point. But there's a basic structure to almost all data visualizations. When we learn to identify these basic structures, we can build our confidence in interpreting and discussing charts.

Follow These Steps

1. Identify the chart title and subtitle: "This chart is titled _____. It is supposed to help us learn _____."
2. Identify the x-axis label: "The x-axis is called _____. This represents _____."
3. Identify the y-axis label: "The y-axis is called _____. This represents _____."
4. If the y-axis contains numbers, identify the scale of the y-axis by naming the lowest number and the highest number: "The y-axis goes from _____ to _____."
5. Describe what the main visual element of the chart represents. What does each bar in a bar chart tell you? What does each point in a dot plot tell you? What does each line in a line chart tell you?

Notes

1. Wexler, Steve, et al. *The Big Book of Dashboards: Visualizing Your Data Using Real-World Business Scenarios.* Wiley, 2017.
2. Healy, Kieran. *Data Visualization: A Practical Introduction.* Princeton University Press, 2019.
3. Evergreen, Stephanie, and Chris Metzner. "Design principles for data visualization in evaluation." *Data visualization, Part 2: New Directions for Evaluation*, Jossey-Bass, 2013, 140, 5–20.
4. Datnow, Amanda, and Vicki Park. *Data-Driven Leadership.* Jossey-Bass, 2014.
5. I don't go into scatter plots in this book because I don't tend to see them as much at the everyday practitioner level. But I do think they're worthwhile to learn. For more, see Goo, Sara Kehaulani. "The Art and Science of the Scatterplot." *Pew*, www.pewresearch.org/fact-tank/2015/09/16/the-art-and-science-of-the-scatterplot/. Accessed 18 March 2021.
6. Fergus, Edward. *Solving Disproportionality and Achieving Equity: A Leader's Guide to Using Data to Change Hearts and Minds.* Corwin, 2016.

7. Knips, Andrew. "6 Steps to Equitable Data Analysis." *Edutopia*, 13 June 2019, www.edutopia.org/article/6-steps-equitable-data-analysis. Accessed 19 March 2021.

8. Schwabish, Jonathan, and Alice Feng. "Applying Racial Equity Awareness in Data Visualization." *OSF Preprints*, 2000. *Urban Institute*, https://urban-institute.medium.com/applying-racial-equity-awareness-in-data-visualization-bd359bf7a7ff. Accessed 29 August 2021.

9. If you make your own visualizations, see this post about the importance of titles: Evergreen, Stephanie. "Strong Titles Are The Biggest Bang for Your Buck." *Evergreen Data*, https://stephanieevergreen.com/strong-titles/. Accessed 29 August 2021.

6

Tables

In This Chapter

In this chapter, you'll learn how to

- ♦ Identify a table
- ♦ Use a question routine to talk about tables
- ♦ Identify the tasks tables help us with
- ♦ Identify the limitations of tables

Suggested Reflection

As you read this chapter, make the learning personal by answering these questions:

- ♦ What's an example of a table you've seen in your daily work?
- ♦ What would it look like, sound like, and feel like to explain that table to a teammate?

DOI: 10.4324/9781003139751-8

Imagine it's summer and you're at the airport, just past the security check. You turn around to see a line of people, faces blank as they load shoes, belts, and laptops into scuffed grey plastic bins. You face forward again and look out at walkways, busy with travelers, some casually rolling their luggage and others speed walking to the next gate.

You feel a nagging sense of urgency that you know will calm as soon as you locate two key pieces of travel information: the gate where your plane departs from and the start time for boarding. Off to the right you spot a large monitor. You walk over and look up at it.

The images on the monitor aren't drastically different from the pictograph tables first made in Mesopotamia—amazing when you consider those were made over five thousand years ago.[1] The monitor shows numbers and words neatly stored in uniformly sized boxes.

The way your eyes scan from top to bottom before landing on the name of your destination city feels automatic, on account

FIGURE 6.1 The airport departures board is an enduring example of a data table. Anything that gets stressed-out travelers to their gate on time has to be good.

of the alphabetic ordering. Your eyes change direction and start traveling left to right, then land on the number of the gate you'll be departing from. Finally, your eyes wander a few more inches to the right, settling on the time your plane leaves.

There's a reason why the preferred data display for busy and stressed out travelers is the data table (Figure 6.1). When done well, data tables organize numbers and words so people can efficiently compare and make associations along rows and columns.[2]

And that's much of what you do with data—compare and make associations. You compare assessment scores to figure out who needs to be in small groups for reteaching. Or you associate times of day with student behavior events. Or maybe you compare student survey results to form recommendations for skill training.

Sometimes the right tool for the job comes in the simplest form, like in tables. And unlike charts that visualize thousands of data points, tables almost always show actual numbers. This gives educators more to reason with.

Out of all the ways you'll learn about sharing data in this book, the one you're most likely to create yourself are tables. Use this chapter to reflect on how tables empower you to make associations and comparisons that aid important decisions. But first, read on for how to identify tables in your everyday work.

How to Spot Tables

There's a sure fire way to know you're looking at a table. All tables look like grids with rows and columns. Ideally, each row is a unique data point. For example, each row could be a student, a school, a district, or a county. Each column contains information about each data point. For example, a column can contain a student's grade level, test score, or the school they attend.

In this example, each row is a school (Table 6.1). There's one column that shows the school's grade levels and there's another column that shows the school's total enrollment.

TABLE 6.1 School Enrollment

Not real data.

School	Grade Level	Total Enrollment
School A	Elementary	435
School B	Secondary	1,783
School C	Secondary	2,532

As with charts, your confidence with tables will grow as you find ways to talk and write about them. To get you started, here's a way you can describe most tables:

> *This table has [NUMBER OF ROWS] rows and [NUMBER OF COLUMNS] columns. Each row is a [DISTRICT, SCHOOL, STUDENT]. Each column gives information about that [DISTRICT, SCHOOL, STUDENT], like [COLUMN TITLE].*

Let's make that more concrete with an example. Here's how we can use this template to describe the school enrollment table example:

> *This table has three rows and three columns. Each row is a school. Each column gives information about that school, like its total enrollment.*

Stay with this example and go a little deeper. When you focus on one row and scan across, you find information associated with that row. When you focus on one column and scan down, you compare the value of that column across different rows.

Scanning across the row for "School A," you find information associated with School A, like the fact that they're an elementary school. And scanning down the column "Grade Level," you find information about grade levels in the table, like the fact there is one elementary school and two secondary schools.

You'll find tables in lots of different places. Researchers use tables to organize their findings in their papers and journal articles. Websites that publish school-related data use them to organize demographic and school performance data. Any time you look at data in a spreadsheet, you're looking at a kind of table.

Sadly, not all tables are created well. Low quality tables are harder to interpret. But starting your approach by identifying a table's parts is a big step towards interpreting and talking about tables confidently.

More Examples of Tables

Now that you've got the vocabulary to describe a table's parts, read through this section to see more examples. As you read through these examples, try writing and saying out loud how you would explain these tables to a teammate.

First, here's an example of a table you'd find from literacy software a school uses as part of reading instruction (Table 6.2). Notice how the title of this table gives you the first big clue about the information inside it. It contains average quiz scores from each grade level at a school:

TABLE 6.2 Average Quiz Score for Each Grade Level in School A

Mean: computed by taking the average of every student's quiz score in each grade level.

Grade	Mean
K	95
1	85
2	75

Here's how I'd describe this table: each row is a unique grade level at the school. I know this because when I scan this small table from top to bottom, I only see each grade level once.

Now contrast this table with the next one, which adds a column that describes when the assessment was taken (Table 6.3):

TABLE 6.3 Average Quiz Score for Each Grade Level in School A

Mean: computed by taking the average of every student's quiz score in each grade level.

Grade	Mean	When
K	95	Start of Year
K	97	End of Year
1	85	Start of Year
1	90	End of Year
2	75	Start of Year
2	76	End of year

Something's changed: each row is no longer a unique grade level at the school. Now when I scan the table from top to bottom, I see grade levels appearing more than once. But when I scan the "Grade" and "When" columns from top to bottom, I see that each row is a unique combination of the "Grade" and "When" columns. Put another way, there are no rows that have the same grade level and test date combination.

If you're just getting started with tables, don't worry if all that feels confusing. The main point is this: learn to recognize how the structure of a table empowers you to make different comparisons. For example, the new "When" column of the second table empowers you to compare quiz results within grades, across grades, and across grades within the same time period.

Challenge yourself to find a table of students, schools, or other topics. When you find one, try describing the table the way I did in this example. Over time, you'll not only find yourself getting more information from tables, but you'll also get better at picking the tables that best support your instructional goals.

What Tables Are Useful For

Stop for a moment and reflect on how much data gets generated in the course of your workday. If you're a teacher, your students create data every time they complete an assignment, take a quiz, or talk to you about how they're doing. If you're a principal, your staff creates data every time they complete a survey, put together a lesson, or give you feedback about the homework policy.

It's hard to keep it all organized. You probably know people that keep quiz scores, notes, student lists, and quarterly assessment results on separate sheets of paper or digital files. And if that person is you, you won't get any judgement from me.

But at some point, most of us realize it's hard to see the big picture when information is spread out everywhere. It's hard for us to use the two powerful analytic tools we've discussed—association and comparison—when the information we have isn't arranged and tidied up.

Tables empower you to compare information by scanning left to right and top to bottom. In a table where each row is a unique student, you can scan a list of quiz scores across students from top to bottom. If that same table has a column that tells you when the student took the quiz, you can pick one student and compare quiz scores from week to week.

Here's the takeaway: if you have information you need to organize so you can compare and make associations, throw it into a table like the ones I've shared in this chapter. You just might find you've got data all around you just waiting to be organized and included in your decision-making process.

Limitations of Tables

So if tables are so great, why aren't we using them all the time?

Our brains and eyes can only handle so much data at once. Recall that tables organize data so we can make comparisons and associations by scanning up and down and left and right. But when there are too many rows and columns, it gets harder for us to take it all in. How many rows and columns are too many? If we have to scroll very far in our spreadsheet application, we might have too much data for us to make sense of.

And it's not just about cognitive processing. There's an emotional element too. Tables that have lots of data can overwhelm us. Researchers have written about the relationship between stress and cognitive performance.[3] When there are so many rows and columns that we feel overwhelmed instead of empowered, we're less likely to access the analytic and creative thinking required for practical data use.

Here's the takeaway: too many rows or columns in a table affects your ability to compare data, which in turn affects your ability to use that data practically. Thankfully, charts and written summaries help you reduce larger datasets down to digestible points so you can use them more practically. See the chapter on charts for more about that.

Equity in Education

A January 2019 article in Brookings showed that schools in the United States with higher percentages of black students also had higher percentages of uncertified teachers.[4] A report by the Sacramento Native American Higher Education Collaborative (SNAHEC) and the Community College Equity Assessment Lab (CCEAL) at San Diego State University showed that, on average, schools in California suspended Native American students at a rate that was more than double the statewide rate.[5] These are only two stories of many about inequality in education.

We need tools to help us discover and share stories about inequality clearly. The tools that work are the ones that empower us to compare outcomes across student groups like racial identity, gender identity, and income. Tables are one such tool because our eyes can scan up and down along student groups to compare outcomes.

Imagine a data table where each row is a student group. Maybe each row is a racial group category, gender identity, low income status, or homeless status. Now imagine that each column is an average outcome for each student group. Maybe there's a column for suspension rates, quiz scores, or attendance rates (Table 6.4):

TABLE 6.4 Example: Key Metrics by Low Income Status
Not Real Data

Low Income Status	Suspension Rate	Average Quiz Score	Attendance Rate
Yes	1 %	87	98%
No	1 %	93	99%

With a table like this, you can scan each outcome from top to bottom across all student groups and ask yourself, are these outcomes similar? If you were a student at your school, how would you feel about your chances there?

These can be difficult questions to ask and answer, especially if that kind of conversation isn't already happening in your school community. Equity data displayed in tables are one way to get that conversation started because they act as external evidence of outcomes for students.

Conclusion

In this chapter, you learned how to identify tables. You also learned about how tables organize information so you can make better associations and comparisons with your data. Armed with this information, you now have concrete ways to approach the tables you encounter in your everyday work. You have new vocabulary and sentences to help you confidently make sense of data tables and lead collaborations where data tables are guiding important decisions for your students.

But data tables are a structure for data, not data itself. In the next chapter, we'll discuss one of the most important kinds of data you'll use in your education job.

Activity: Making Your Own Tables

What This Does
This activity helps you learn how to use tables to organize information and investigate school outcomes across student groups.

How This Can Help Us
It takes both personal stories and data to understand and act on inequality in our schools. When we listen to stories and observe the experiences of our students, we get clues about what inequality might look like in our schools. Then, we can look at classroom, school or district data in tables to learn more.

Instructions
- ◆ Review the sample table below (Table 6.5). In this table, each row is a student group. Each column contains an outcome for each student group
- ◆ Complete this table for your school
- ◆ For each column, scan the outcomes for each group and discuss differences with teammates. What stories from your own experiences come up for you as you look at this table?
- ◆ Modify the table to include different student groups, like gender identity or free and reduced lunch status
- ◆ Modify the table to include different student outcomes, like weekly assessment scores

TABLE 6.5 Outcomes by Student Group (Consider race, gender identity, or socio-economic status)

Student Group	Suspension Rate	Attendance Rate	State Testing Math	State Testing Language Arts
Student Group 1				
Student Group 2				
Student Group 3				
Student Group 4				
Student Group 5				
Student Group 6				
Student Group 7				

Notes

1. Hirst, Kris K. "Proto-Cuneiform: Earliest Form of Writing on Planet Earth." *ThoughtCo*, 27 March 2019, www.thoughtco.com/proto-cuneiform-earliest-form-of-writing-171675. Accessed 1 July 2021.
2. Sometimes rows go by other names, like "observations" and columns go by other names like "variables."
3. Lupien, S. J. "The effects of stress and stress hormones on human cognition: Implications for the field of brain and cognition." *Brain and Cognition*, 2007, www.sciencedirect.com/science/article/abs/pii/S0278262607000322. Accessed 1 July 2021.
4. Startz, Dick. "Equal opportunity in American education: In memory of Martin Luther King Jr." *Brookings*, 15 January 2019, www.brookings.edu/blog/brown-center-chalkboard/2019/01/15/equal-opportunity-in-american-education/. Accessed 1 July 2021.
5. Hong, Joe. "Study: California's Native American Students Suspended, Expelled At Higher Rates." *KPBS*, 3 October 2019, www.kpbs.org/news/2019/oct/03/study-native-american-students-suspended-expelled-/. Accessed 1 July 2021.

7

Student-Level Data

In This Chapter

In this chapter, you'll learn how to

+ Identify student-level data
+ Identify challenges when using student-level data
+ Use student-level data in combination with aggregate data

Suggested Reflection

As you read this chapter, make the learning personal by answering these questions:

+ Which student-level datasets do you find yourself using often?
+ How can you combine student-level data with school-level and district-level data to learn more about the unique experiences of your students?

DOI: 10.4324/9781003139751-9

    ◆   If you needed to share student-level data with a team-mate, what procedures would you follow to protect the privacy of your students?

The other day, I thought about how I say the word "data" a hundred times a day and get away with not explaining what I mean by it. That didn't seem like a big deal until I realized it wasn't a practical way to talk with other educators about data. That's because what data means is different for everyone, depending on the kind of work they do.

Krista, a middle school teacher, reminded me of this when she shared her stories with me in the fall of 2020. Krista was part of the student success team, a team of educators at her school site that developed interventions for students who needed a little more instructional support.

Given the goals of the student success team, Krista needed data that helped her understand the changing needs of her students on a daily basis:

> That's the difference between end-of-year testing data and [more frequent] student success team data. With student success team data you're looking at the student in real time. You're asking questions like, "What's the problem?" and "Can we come up with a game plan?"

If end-of-year test scores are the yearly physical at the doctor's office, then student success teams are our friends and family asking us every week, "How are you feeling? And is there anything we can do to help?" If we ask these types of questions more often, it's much better for our health. And basing all our health decisions on a yearly physical seems quite precarious indeed.

Krista fully embraced the benefits of the student success team, and she made practical use of data by matching it to its best function. Put another way, Krista knew the best data for the student success team was student-level data.

How to Spot Student-Level Data

The telltale sign that you're looking at student-level data is the existence of personally identifiable student information. It's the thing that makes student data a powerful resource for decision-making. It's also the thing that requires you to be mindful of privacy, safety, and appropriate use. Your organization likely has rules and procedures for sharing student-level data. And if it doesn't, consider leading the charge to create them.

So far, we've talked about charts and tables. Both of these come in the student-level variety. You'll know that's what you have when you see that the data is at the student level, as opposed to the school level or district level.

Consider a table of student-level data, where each row in the table represents one student and the columns contain data associated with that student. Or consider a bar chart, where each bar represents one student and the length of that bar is the count of some event for that student.

You'll mostly find student-level data where they're generated—in schools and school districts. Teachers use student-level data from their classrooms. School principals use student-level data from their schools. And school districts use student-level data from their district. But outside of these settings, student-level data is harder to come by (more on that later in the chapter). So if you have access to it, you'll have a somewhat rare source of information to support your decision-making.

Examples of Student-Level Data

When some educators think of data, they think of formal data sources, like statewide testing results. It's true that student-level data comes in formal flavors, like standardized assessments.

But it's not the only kind of student-level data educators have. And for some, it might not even be the most useful. That's because classroom teachers and principals make frequent decisions, sometimes many in one day. So they need data that comes just as frequently and in easily interpretable forms.

Here are some examples of student-level data. Notice how some of these are formal and some of these are less formal:

- Student cumulative files
- Notes from a parent conference
- Exit ticket assessments
- Thumbs up/thumbs down quick assessments
- Writing samples
- Weekly quizzes
- Quarterly formative assessments
- End-of-year summative assessments

Can you think of others? Take a moment to open your notebook and brainstorm other sources of student-level data, both formal and informal. You might discover that you have more student-level data around you than you originally thought.

What Student-Level Data Is Useful For

If we define practical as something you can do in your classroom tomorrow, then the most practical kind of data is student-level data. Student-level data gives you information about an individual student to help you make decisions for that individual student.

This kind of data can point you to the stories that help you understand what your students need on a highly individualized level. This empowers you to go beyond the numbers and into the student stories that reveal individual needs.

Consider this example, which compares group data, also known as aggregate data, with student-level data. As you follow along, reflect on how changing from aggregate data to individualized data expands what you can learn about the students.

Here's a table of average assessment scores for five third grade classrooms (Table 7.1). Being group data, this table helps us compare performances across groups of students. In this case, the table displays average scores across classrooms:

TABLE 7.1 Assessment Scores for Five Classrooms

The score is the average of all student scores in the classroom. Student scores are a percentage of assessment items correct.

Classroom	Average Score
1	82
2	86
3	69
4	78
5	71

But aggregate data does not allow us to go deep on a particular student or understand the spread of scores within each classroom. For that, you'll need student-level data (Table 7.2):

TABLE 7.2 Assessment Scores for Students in Classroom 1

Student scores are a percentage of assessment items correct.

Name	Classroom	Score
Sarah	1	75
Frank	1	95
Sofia	1	63
Michael	1	85
Natalie	1	92

Zooming in on one student's data is like following a bread crumb that leads you to more useful questions: "Sarah was one of two students that scored below 80 percent on that last assessment. Let's look at her work to see what's happening."

Now you know the benefits of student-level data. Let's now discuss some of its limitations.

Limitations of Student-Level Data

Student-level data gives you parts of a student's story. It's the most individualized information educators can get. So why shouldn't all data be this way? Let's explore two reasons why student-level data has its limits.

You Have to Generalize Student-Level Data

Even if you understand each and every one of your students, you still have to plan efficient ways to meet their needs in groups. It comes down to a tension that practical data users are up against all the time: the more individualized data gets, the harder it is to apply what you learned to help many students at once. Let's unpack that a little more.

Let's say a third-grade teacher has a classroom of 25 students. That teacher has a dataset of each student's scores from last week's assessment on decimals. If she tried to make 25 individualized programs for each student in response to each weekly assessment, she'd find out pretty quickly that she won't have time for much else.

Even though student-level data gives you the most information about individual students, you still need to group students before that information is usable in a daily or weekly routine. When you have a lot of student-level data, make time to find themes and patterns that appear across the student data. You'll need those patterns to plan how to reach as many students as you can with what you've learned.

Student Privacy

In order to protect the privacy of our students, we can only share student-level data with people who are allowed to use it. Usually this means students, parents, teachers, and site administration. As educators, we're still figuring out good ways to balance our access to student data for improving instruction against respecting the privacy of students and their families. In recent years, states have proposed and passed laws that try to make sense of how to do this well.[1]

This limited sharing could also mean a slower exchange of ideas with educators outside your school or district.

Contrast that with publicly available data, which can be shared with anyone, requiring little or no procedures to do so. Most of the time it's as easy as emailing or texting a link to a website.

For example, if I wanted to share a publicly available chart about attendance in a local school district, I can just paste the link in an email and send it. On the other hand, it's different if I wanted to share a chart of a student's decreasing behavior referrals. Depending on the school district's policy, I could probably only share that with you if we worked at the same school. And even then, there might be rules against emailing it to you.

I've done and seen interesting ways to share student-level data in a way that protects students. Anonymizing the data is one way to do that. Having carefully written data agreements and procedures for sharing is another way.[2]

The practical takeaway here is this: while student-level data has its obvious advantages for decision-making, it shouldn't be the only thing you use in your data routines. Having a variety of go-to data sources will give you much-needed context for student-level data. It will also give you options when student-level data isn't available.

Equity in Education

In order to understand how student-level data helps us connect to equity in schools, we first have to understand the close cousin of student-level data: aggregate data. In contrast to student-level data, aggregate data is data that groups students together. Rather than measuring outcomes for individual students, aggregate data measures outcomes for groups of students.

Total enrollment numbers, percent of students who scored in the proficient range on a test, and percent of students suspended by race group are all aggregate datasets. We can use aggregate data to describe average outcomes for student groups, like racial groups, gender identity, or income level. But there's a downside to analyzing student group outcomes: we lose the story of the individual student.

For example, aggregate data might show us that foster students in our school district have lower attendance rates on average. But how well can we describe what that experience is like for a specific student, and how that affects different parts of their school experience?

Student-level data helps by pointing us towards the stories of individual students. This kind of data empowers us to ask questions like Who is this student who is thriving and what is their story? Or Who is this student who is struggling and what is their story?

Ideally, the solution is to combine aggregate data and student-level data to build a more complete picture of what our students need. That way, we have group-level data that shows us inequality in our system and we have student-level data that shows us the individual stories of our students. This combination speaks to both the mind and the heart. And it also reminds us that, while many individual stories are captured in aggregate data, our students still need us to hear and understand their individual experiences.

Conclusion

Focusing on the student-level experience is the north star of our work. It's the thing we all care about, no matter how procedural our jobs get or no matter how different our opinions are about the right way to get things done.

In this chapter, you learned how to dig deep into the student-level experience by going from aggregate data to student-level data. You also learned how student-level data is not without its drawbacks.

To round things out, we'll close the field guide section of *The K-12 Educator's Data Guidebook* with another kind of data source. This data source gets a bad rap with educators and yet there's no sign it's going away. Got your attention? Read on for more.

Activity: Student-Level Data Organizer

What This Does

This activity shows you how to organize student-level data so you're ready to make decisions at the right time.

How This Can Help Us

Time is one of the main challenges, if not *the* main challenge, that prevents us from using data practically in our everyday work. You can save time by planning so you have everything you need to make a data-informed decision when the time comes.

When it's time to make your daily, weekly, or monthly decisions, you want your student-level data sources organized and ready to review. This organizer will help you get from data to decision quickly (Table 7.3).

Instructions

1. Start your organizer by creating a three-column list in a notebook or spreadsheet. The first column will contain your student-level data sources. The second column will contain decisions you need to make. The third column will contain how often you make that decision.
2. Earlier in the chapter, we brainstormed a list of student-level data sources. Review that list and enter the ones you use, plus any other ideas you have, into the "Student-Level Data Source" column.

TABLE 7.3 Example of Student-Level Data Sources

Student-Level Data Source	Decision	Frequency
Exit ticket	Plan small groups	Weekly
Observations from teacher journal	Plan individual check-in	Twice a week
Weekly quiz results	Plan reteach	Weekly
Student study team forms	Plan grade level meeting	Monthly

3. Review each student-level data source and write down a matching decision in the "Decision" column.
4. Write down how often you make each decision in the "Frequency" column.
5. Before you make each decision, commit to reviewing your organizer for a few minutes to find and review student-level data that supports your decision-making process.

Notes

1. The Data Quality Campaign. "State Student Data Privacy Legislation: What Happened in 2014, and What Is Next?" *The Data Quality Campaign*, 22 September 2014, https://dataqualitycampaign.org/resource/state-student-data-privacy-legislation-happened-2014-next/. Accessed 29 August 2021.
2. This is part of a practice called "data governance," in case you ever hear that term. In my opinion, it's one of the most important and underrated practices we can do to build a strong data culture in schools. For more on data governance, see Geller, Wendy, et al. *Education Data Done Right: Lessons from the Trenches of Applied Data Science.* Independently published, 2019.

8

Accountability Data

In This Chapter

In this chapter, you'll learn how to

- ◆ Identify accountability data
- ◆ Use accountability data as context for school level and student-level data
- ◆ Identify the limitations of accountability data
- ◆ Use accountability data as a tool for promoting equity

Suggested Reflection

As you read this chapter, make the learning personal by answering these questions:

- ◆ Which accountability datasets do you see often in your everyday work?
- ◆ How can you combine accountability data with student-level data to learn more about the unique experiences of your students?

DOI: 10.4324/9781003139751-10

♦ What emotions come up for you as you view accountability data, especially with high stakes data like end-of-year testing?

As I write this book, I'm at the start of my twentieth year working in public education. And for as long as I've worked in public education, accountability data—data whose main purpose is to track a target—has been there with me. It's like the basket of unfolded laundry I have upstairs in the bedroom. I'd prefer to deal with other things, but not tending to it would be negligence of a basic duty.

Accountability data is a purpose driven kind of data, as all good data should be. Your practical use of it depends on how many of your job responsibilities are aimed at accountability and compliance. A superintendent will spend more time with accountability data than a classroom aide will, for example.

So since accountability data isn't going away, we might as well learn how to use it. Afterall, that laundry isn't going to fold itself.

How to Spot Accountability Data

The first way to spot accountability data is to look for group-level data. Remember in the last chapter when we talked about student-level data? That's the kind where each datapoint represents a student. Accountability data is different. Datapoints in accountability rarely represent individual students. They almost always represent groups of students, like schools, districts, counties, or states.

The second way to spot accountability data is to look for what's measured. In the last chapter, we looked at how student-level data gives us information about the experiences of students in the classroom. Again, accountability data is different. It measures events in education that one agency needs to report to another agency (hence, the "accountability" part of accountability). Look for columns in these datasets that explicitly measure an event that a school or district is accountable for.

Here's are some examples of accountability data:

◆ A list of each school district's attendance rate, created by the state education agency

◆ A report of special education identification rates at each school by student race groups, created by a school district

◆ A website that shows the percent of students at a school who were proficient in math and English language arts, created by a school district

None of these examples contain datapoints of individual students. Instead, each datapoint is a group of students. And all of these examples measure some event that gets reported to another party for accountability. Let's look closer at a couple of examples.

Example 1: State Testing

Here's an arbitrary example I made with fake data, similar to what you'd find on the National Assessment of Educational Progress (NAEP) website (Table 8.1).[1]

Data like this is collected and reported so states can be accountable to the public for their test performance scores. Data like this won't help everyday educators make decisions about their daily practice—there are much better ways to do that, as we've discussed in previous chapters.[2] But it can serve as context for the test scores of students in their schools and classrooms.

TABLE 8.1 Distance from the National Average Test Score by State

Not real data.

State	Average Score	Distance From National Average	At or Above Proficient
State A	250	0	49
State B	255	+5	52
State C	256	+6	53
State D	262	+12	57
State E	267	+17	60

As with all data reporting, your practical interpretation will improve when you understand what each column means.[3] I encourage you to read through the dataset's documentation, which you can usually find on the website where you found the data. It's about as exciting as filing a tax return, but I promise it will help you interpret data like this accurately and more practically.

In this example, you'll need to know that the "Average Score" column is the average score of all students in the state who took this test. You'll also need to know that the possible range of scores goes from 0 to 500.

You can interpret a row in this accountability dataset like this: "Students in State A scored 250 on average. This was the same as what students across the country scored, on average. In State A, 49 percent of the students who took the test scored in the proficient range or higher."

Example 2: College Readiness

Here's another arbitrary example I made, again with fake data (Table 8.2). You can find publicly available data about college preparedness on state educational agency websites like the California Department of Education.[4] In this example, I used generic student group labels, like "Student Group 1." When you see accountability data in the wild, student group labels will be more specific. Some examples of student groups are racial groups, socio-economic status, foster status, or homelessness status.

TABLE 8.2 College Preparedness by Student Group

	Student Group 1	Student Group 2	Student Group 3
Percentage Prepared	47.7 %	48.3%	46.2%
Percentage Approaching Prepared	15.2%	16.3%	17.2%
Percentage Not Prepared	37.1%	35.4%	36.6%

Datasets like this are designed to report on how many students are adequately prepared for college, based on some set criteria for preparedness.

Again, reviewing the technical documentation for datasets like this pays off when you interpret and communicate what you've learned. For example, the technical documentation for the college and career preparedness data in California tells us that preparedness is defined by a number of criteria.[5] Some examples of preparedness are completing a sequence of courses, performance levels on end-of-year testing, and results of other exams.

Using this information, let's interpret one row of data: "About 48 percent of students in group 1 met the criteria for college and career readiness as defined by our state education agency. About 48 percent of students in group 2 met the criteria and about 46 percent of students in group 3 met the criteria."

What Accountability Data Is Useful For

When I go to the grocery store, I feel overwhelmed by the amount of stuff that's in there. The only thing stopping me from descending into a pit of irreversible confusion is the fact that items are grouped under somewhat arbitrary categories: frozen foods, meats, things that come from cows and chickens, and processed comfort foods. With those categories, I can stand outside the building and say, "This is a grocery store." Without those categories, I'm standing in front of a building full of a lot of stuff. If I go in there, am I buying milk or sneakers?

As much as accountability data has gotten a bad rap amongst educators, it does come with its advantages.[6] And it all comes down to learning from patterns that exist in large volumes of data. The categories used in accountability data empowers us to zoom out and see patterns, just like the categories in the grocery stores empower us to understand what items we'll find in them.

See, we can think about improving the school experience on different levels, like in small groups, in a classroom, at a school, and in the community. But as the number of students at each level gets larger and larger it gets harder and harder to pick out the patterns that matter.

While accountability data is rarely a complete story of a student's or a school's outcomes, it can act as context for local data. When we combine accountability data with local data, we get more detailed answers for questions like: are we improving how our students learn the math standards? Are we improving how consistently students are in classrooms, ready to learn? And are we relying more on community building for addressing behaviors and less on suspensions?

Let's look at an example. Consider this analytic statement about some imaginary end-of-year testing dataset for one school:

> Our school's performance on the summative assessment was 10 points higher than last year.

Now consider the same statement, but with added context from a larger accountability dataset:

> Our school's performance on the summative assessment was 10 points higher than last year. The average change in scores across our district was about 7 points.

In the second statement, accountability data is used to put local results in the context of some larger result. This helps educators understand local results with more nuance. In this example, the second statement doesn't just show that this year's scores were higher than last year's. It also suggests that the change was higher than the district's average change.

Limitations of Accountability Data

If you're reading this book from the first chapter, you're probably noticing a pattern in the way I see things: the way to keep data in schools practical is to expand. Expand your personal stories about data, expand the kinds of data you look at, and even expand what you consider data in the first place.

When we don't expand how we think about data, we're left with a limited selection of data sources. And from my experience, any single data source is not as good as multiple data sources.

This is especially true of accountability data. Accountability data are designed to answer questions about accountability. Unless you're the person responsible for reporting accountability results to a state or federal agency, accountability data probably won't be the most useful data for your kind of decision-making. This data, while extremely important for its own purposes, is not likely to reflect the questions you need to answer. Have a look at these examples, which starts with a practical question, shows a related accountability dataset, and suggests a better alternative (Table 8.3).

Accountability data are collected infrequently, tend to be quantitative, and usually represent a snapshot in time. On its own, that doesn't tend to build a full enough picture for daily decision-making. But it can give helpful context to data that is collected more frequently, has a mix of quantitative and qualitative sources, and represents changes over time.

TABLE 8.3 Examples of Accountability Data and Better Alternatives

Practical Question	Accountability Data	Better Alternative
Are my students present for instruction every day?	Rates of chronic absenteeism	Daily attendance records
Are my students learning fractions?	Percent proficient on end-of-year testing	Weekly math quizzes
Does the local community feel connected and invested in the school?	End-of-year community safety survey results	Theme analysis of notes from monthly coffee with principals talk

Equity in Education

Defining equity in student outcomes isn't such a straightforward thing. We can approach that question from different angles. Do students more or less have an equal chance of participating in school activities? Do students more or less have an equal opportunity to meet their full potential? Are students shown respect for who they are, no matter what their background?

Accountability data aimed at equity-related goals helps us set targets that, while not describing the full complexity of equitable school outcomes, still give us a piece of what equity means in schools. Suspension rates by racial group, attendance rate by gender identity, and formative assessment results by socioeconomic status are all examples of accountability data that gives us clues about the state of equity at our school.

If you're an education leader who works with accountability datasets like the ones I described, help build awareness about equity by learning and communicating how districts, counties, and state agencies define it in their data collection. Ask questions like:

- What are the data collection requirements for suspensions?
- How are absence rates calculated?
- What metrics are used for special education identification rates?
- And perhaps most importantly, which student groups are included in required datasets—are racial groups, gender identity, and income-related groups included?

Indeed, leaders play an important role in practical data use because they can help bridge the gap between abstract measurements and how classroom staff provide instruction in day-to-day work.

Equity work, like any work, requires action to move towards the vision we have for our students. Discovering that action with accountability data is a more complex task than with more practical workaday measures like running records and exit tickets. But with collaboration, discussion, and creativity, we can use accountability data to clarify how we can take an abstract idea like equity and turn it into something practical. We'll explore one way to do that in the activity section of this chapter.

Conclusion

In this chapter, you learned about what accountability data is designed for. You also learned how you can use it to give context to school level or student-level data.

This chapter concludes the field guide section of this book. But what good is all this data if we don't have some consistent way to use it? In the next section, we'll learn practical ways to use this data in our everyday work.

Activity: Turning Accountability Data Into Local Data

What This Does
In this activity, you'll be reflecting on the connections between accountability data and school or classroom data.

How This Can Help Us
Accountability data is designed to describe some accountability event, like end-of-year test scores, school climate, attendance, or discipline. For everyday educators, the larger scale and obscure measurements of accountability data make it hard to see how accountability data is helpful for everyday decisions. This activity helps us make a connection between accountability data and school-level or student-level data.

Instructions
For this activity, you'll need an accountability dataset from a state local agency or from the US Department of Education's

website. These datasets are publicly available and are free to download. You'll also need accountability data from your own school or school district. This local data should roughly mirror the data collected by the state local agency or the federal government.

- ◆ Review an accountability dataset from a state educational agency
- ◆ Identify the columns and their definitions
- ◆ Create a new spreadsheet with these same columns. Alternatively, list the columns on a sheet of paper
- ◆ Use your local data to create a dataset that resembles the state agency or US federal government dataset
- ◆ Reflect individually or as a team: how is your dataset similar or different from the state agency's dataset? How would you include these details in the stories you share with your community?

Let's look at an example. We'll go back to our accountability dataset from earlier in the chapter (see Table 8.1), which tells us the average end-of-year testing score for five states:

We can take these same columns and create a worksheet. This worksheet will help us organize our own data using the state education agency's format. We can enter data from our school, including data like racial groups, gender, or an income-related field. Here's an example (Table 8.4). Notice how the columns

TABLE 8.4 Distance from the National Average Test Score by Student Group Not real data.

	Average Score	Distance From National Average	At or Above Proficient
Our School	?	?	?
Student Group 1	?	?	?
Student Group 2	?	?	?
Student Group 3	?	?	?
Student Group 4	?	?	?

mirror the columns in the accountability dataset. What's different about this new table is that it has data for a school instead of states.

You can find local data like this at your school site. In some cases, the agency that produces the accountability dataset also provides data by school and student groups.

Building a table like this is a good way to bridge from the abstract nature of big accountability datasets to the more practical nature of school or student-level datasets.

Notes

1. National Assessment of Educational Progress. "How Did U.S. Students Perform On the Most Recent Assessments?" *The Nation's Report Card*, www.nationsreportcard.gov. Accessed 29 August 2021.
2. See Chapter 7, Student-Level Data.
3. For a more thorough discussion of rows and columns, see chapter 7, Tables.
4. California Department of Education. "School Dashboards Additional Reports and Data." *California Department of Education*, www6.cde.ca.gov/californiamodel/. Accessed 29 August 2021.
5. California Department of Education. "College/Career Readiness Calculation." *California Department of Education*, www.cde.ca.gov/ta/ac/cm/ccical.asp. Accessed 29 August 2021.
6. See Chapter 2, "Why Tests Aren't Enough."

Part 3
Process Made Practical

I noticed something about the way my wife and I cook together. She's at a much higher skill level than me, so I move slower than she does. She's well practiced, so she uses her muscle memory to move quickly. And she does so while answering many questions from me ("Am I doing this right?").

But I have found one thing that helps me keep up: meal prep services. You know the ones I mean. Those services that send you everything you need to prepare a meal: perfectly measured ingredients, detailed instructions written in a friendly and welcoming tone, and photographs of the final presentation.

How can meal prep services make me competent in the kitchen in a way that plain old recipes haven't? Put simply, the meal prep services give me concrete steps to follow. Following these steps helps me feel less overwhelmed. They also facilitate a result, which in turn builds my confidence. In time, I'll have the level of skill required to work from instinct and to improvise. But for now, using these steps is a way to mentally organize the chaos.

This section describes steps everyday educators can use to work with data. The chapters in this section are designed to relieve the feelings of stress and ambiguity educators sometimes feel in the face of new data.

Read this if:

♦ Using data feels overwhelming and you're looking for steps to follow

DOI: 10.4324/9781003139751-11

- You have a good process for working with data, but have trouble describing it
- You feel like data use is disconnected from your everyday work life
- You use data, but don't have a process to see what's working

Activities in This Section

You'll find these activities at the end of each chapter in this section:

1. Improve These Data Questions.
2. Making Meaning Out of Data in Three Steps.
3. Reflecting on Job Duties, Decisions, and Data.
4. How to Get Feedback by Email.

9

Using Data Questions

In This Chapter

In this chapter, you'll learn learn about

♦ Why we should lead our analytic routines with questions that matter to us
♦ A list of questions to help you clarify what you want from the data in front of you
♦ An example of asking and answering data questions

Suggested Reflection

As you read this chapter, make the learning personal by answering these questions:

♦ Where in your personal life do you use data effectively and confidently?
♦ Staying with examples in your personal life, what are the useful questions you answer using data?

DOI: 10.4324/9781003139751-12

- ◆ How can you apply similar thinking to data use in your education job?

Imagine it's your first day on the job at an elementary school. The students are showing up in three days fresh from summer break and ready to tackle the first day of the year (or not—you can write that part of the story).[1] It's the start of the school year, so the principal is going from classroom to classroom handing out manila folders. You open your folder and find writing, graphs, and tables describing the results from last school year's end-of-year state testing. There's a cover letter from the principal. She starts the letter by saying she hopes your summer was renewing. And she ends by asking you to review the data in preparation for a staff meeting at the end of the day.

Situations like these are common in schools. When someone gives you information and asks you what you think about it, it can cause all kinds of feelings. Stress and avoidance are two that come to mind for me. As with any task that has ambiguous goals, not knowing where to start can stop you from starting at all.

Think of other situations in your life that cause similar feelings: planning your child's birthday party, starting your taxes, or purging stuff out of your garage. How do we deal with those situations so we can calm our overwhelm and begin moving through a process?

One way is to add just a little bit of structure to the picture so it feels less chaotic. We make a list of people to invite to the party, we send an email to our accountant asking about the next step for filing taxes, and we sort the mess in our garage into things to keep and things to donate. In other words, we apply some organizing principles that can help us focus on the steps we need to take.

In this chapter, we'll explore a powerful organizing principle for analyzing data: data questions. And here's the good news: through our professional experiences and collaboration with others, we've got all the questions we need to make our data use matter for our students. Let's get started.

A Practical Definition

Here's how I define a data question:

> *A data question is a sentence we write before looking at data. We use this question to guide the kind of data we look for and how we interpret it. A good data question helps us make important decisions, encourages us to think broadly, guides us to the right data, and helps us find timely answers.*

Teachers and administrators in schools have all kinds of data available to them for decision-making. The amount of data is dizzying—educators see everything from informal data like notes from student conferences to quantitative data like the kind found in academic research papers. It can all be very overwhelming, like going to a restaurant with a menu that's got a hundred entrees on it. Which do you go with? I use data questions to cope with the stress I feel when I need to make some decisions in the face of a lot of information.

Imagine your last trip to the local library. How do you pick books from such a vast selection? You can start by wandering around and exploring, but at some point you'll need to get clear on what you want to learn or enjoy before you start picking books and reading.

It's the same for educators when they've got a decision to make and lots of data to look at. A good data question is the quickest path to clarity. In fact, when my teammates ask me "Can you help me look at this data?" I always respond with "What's the question you're trying to answer?"

So let's talk about what makes a data question good so you can use it as a tool to bring confidence and focus to how you use data. You'll know a data question is good when:

♦ It helps you make a decision that is directly connected to your goal as an educator

- ◆ It is broad enough that you need to look at more than one source of information to answer it
- ◆ It is specific enough that it helps you tell the difference between relevant and irrelevant data
- ◆ It's answerable on the right timeline for your job—daily, monthly, or yearly

If we can train ourselves to apply these four qualities to the way we ask questions, we'll be well on our way to using our data practically. Let's look at each of these a little closer.

Helps You Make the Right Decisions

When I first started as a district office administrator back in 2007, I got to meet the team that organized transportation for students. In the summer of that year, I stopped by the transportation office, which was housed in a portable building nearby. Once inside, I said hello to the department director, Kyra (not her real name).

Kyra brought me over to a computer, where she showed me how she organized efficient routes for students taking the bus from their home to campus. She used software to visualize maps, routes, neighborhoods, and other related data. She calmly and professionally walked me through each report, uncovering the intricate system of decisions needed to make all of this work.

Where did Kyra's confidence with transportation data come from? I believe it came from the practical connection between the data she used and the decisions she needed to make to accomplish her job. There was no requirement to look at data that didn't help the cause of the transportation department, which was to safely deliver students from home to school and back.

This was Kyra's data question: what is the most efficient and safest route between home and school for each student? This data question brought perfect clarity to how Kyra picked her data and how she used it.

Have you ever thought to yourself "I could teach this lesson better if I knew which part isn't connecting with my students?" or "I can plan professional development better if I knew what teachers thought about the last training?" Listen to these thoughts. They're the voice of your professional intuition pointing you to good data questions. And when you uncover the right questions, you take a step closer to using data to answer them.

Broad Enough to Require Multiple Sources of Data

Sylvia, a vice principal at an elementary school, organizes time for teachers to review data about what their students are learning. During these data review sessions, Sylvia and the teachers take a common approach to understanding what their students learned: they look at statewide testing scores: "We take all these yearly test results and we look at where we made gains. We ask What do you see in this data? What do you think about it? And what's next?"

But Sylvia believes that learning how many students scored in the "proficient" range is only one part of their story. To understand the rest of the story, Sylvia goes to other sources of data: "The percent proficient just gives you the big picture. We have to look at the individual class data for these tests."

While I listened to Sylvia tell her story, she reminded me of someone tending to their garden. They start by looking at what's growing. Then they look at the topsoil. Then, wanting to know even more, they go beneath the topsoil. Sylvia starts with statewide testing, but digs all the way down to the school, classroom, and student levels. At the student level, Sylvia and the teachers look at all kinds of data sources to learn about who needs more of their time, attention, and creativity.

This style of data use becomes possible when we ask data questions that require broad investigation (though not too broad, as we'll see in the next section). For Sylvia, that question is "Which students need more of our time, attention, and creativity?" This is a question about students, not about data. And because of that, the question leads Sylvia and the teachers to many sources of information.

Consider these data questions that require broad investigation:

- How well are we teaching fractions to our students?
- Are we applying our discipline procedures fairly?
- Do parents feel like a part of our school community?

Contrast those with data questions that keep you locked into one source of data:

- What percent of students passed the fractions quiz?
- What's our suspension rate?
- What was the lowest scoring survey item?

If you're feeling stuck with your data use, try going broader with your data questions. It just might point you to meaningful data you would have otherwise missed.

Specific Enough to Help You Narrow Down Your Data

This is where good data questions start to feel more like art than science. As I mentioned in the last section, the broader your data question, the more opportunities there are to discover useful data. But is there such a thing as too broad? Let's explore more with a hypothetical example.

Imagine Rashaad is a principal at a K–6 elementary school. Rashaad wants to improve attendance at his elementary school. He's decided to start by researching the baseline levels of attendance. What are some ways he can frame attendance at his school as a question?

Rashaad could start with something like this: *What were the attendance totals for today on the student system report?* This is a little too narrow. If Rashaad starts with this question, he'll get stuck in a pretty small conversation about attendance. Rashaad could track this daily number over time and look for changes, but that would leave out opportunities to learn about how to improve attendance. A narrow question like this is less likely to lead Rashaad to other interesting data. Notes from a staff meeting where teachers built a system map for the attendance process, a review of attendance slip documentation, and conversations with students are all sources of data that would contribute to a fuller story about attendance.

How about something broader: *Are the students happy at school?* This is a little too broad. If Rashaad starts with this question, it will be hard for him to efficiently identify the attendance-related data that matters. He might even end up with a presentation slide deck that talks about student happiness. That deck would have inspiring stories, but it probably wouldn't address the topic of attendance specifically enough. That's because questions that are too broad don't encourage enough intentionality about which data sources to pick.

And now the Goldilocks of data questions, something not too narrow and not too broad: *In general, how would we describe the state of attendance at our school?* This gets really interesting. Let's look at why.

First, it's broad enough to guide us towards multiple data sources. The state of attendance can be described by last year's attendance rates, daily attendance rates over time, parent interviews, student interviews, and a review of the current attendance process. And second, it's specific enough to keep us focused on attendance-related data. So if Rashaad is reviewing a community survey that's fifty items long, he'll know to sort and focus on the attendance-related questions.

Feeling like your data question is leading you on a wild goose chase? Try dialing it down to a narrower topic. You'll know when you've got just the right balance when you discover multiple data sources to investigate and they all feel focused on the question.

Answerable on the Right Timeline

Imagine if your banking website showed you your checking account balance just once a year. On the special day when you receive your yearly balance, you sit down with your morning cup of coffee. You fire up your bank's website and look at how the bottom line is doing. Oops! Looks like you spent too much on coffee last year. You look glumly at your morning cup and resolve to spend less on coffee. You draft a plan to buy one less coffee a week, then proceed to keep your under-caffeinated fingers crossed for the remaining twelve months, at which point you will again view your checking account balance.

This would never work. Why? Because managing cash flow requires decisions on a daily or weekly basis. To make good personal finance decisions, you need data at least that often. It's the same with good data questions. You need to craft questions so they're answerable when you need to make a decision, and no later than that.

Remember Sylvia from earlier in the chapter? During our conversation, Sylvia believes one downside to yearly testing is that . . . well, it only comes yearly. That means Sylvia's team can only check on how things are going once a year.

In the same way we rely on our banking website to have daily or weekly reports, Sylvia and her teachers rely on more frequent measures of English language arts and math. These include tests designed by their school district, assessments from software programs, and teacher-designed quizzes. Notice the variety here. There's data about English language arts and math from different sources, and each source arrives at different frequencies.

How often do you need to make an important decision? It depends on your job. A teacher makes data-informed decisions on a daily basis, like making adjustments to the next day's lesson plans. A school principal might look at, among other things, formative assessments that come every quarter. That helps evaluate medium-term strategies her team is trying. And a district office administrator might look at a year's worth of data to begin leading a conversation about a school district's goals for the following year.

There's one last point I want to make about time horizons. It's an observation I've made while experimenting with data use in my professional and personal life. The more frequently data appears, the less formal it tends to be. The less frequently data appears, the more formal it *can* be.

This isn't a hard and fast rule, but it does seem to make sense. If you need to decide who to give one-on-one support to every other hour, your data source might be a show of hands from your students to check for understanding. On the other hand, if you need to decide on a formal strategy to improve school district attendance rates next school year, your data source might be formal reporting from student data systems.

Here's my advice: care less about how fancy the data is and care more about how connected the data is to the decision at hand. Keep doing that, and you'll be just fine.

Conclusion

As you travel along your path towards meaningful data use, you'll likely find yourself exploring lots of sources of data. This is good, because it means you're exposing yourself to new forms of external information. Before you know it, you'll begin forming tight connections between that information, your professional intuition, and the decisions you make to help your students.

In this chapter, you learned that all this new information can lead to feelings of stress. And importantly, you learned that good data questions are the lifesaver you need when you feel like you're drowning in a deluge of datapoints.

In the next chapter, you'll learn how to calmly wade through those datapoints, generating even more questions and ideas as you explore them for meaning.

Activity: Improve These Data Questions

Use this activity to practice making and recognizing good data questions.

How This Helps Us

Making good data questions is a skill people learn much faster if they practice regularly and with teammates. This can be used by many educator roles—teachers, administrators, or district office staff. Don't be afraid to try the activity with other people who do the same job as you and also with people who do jobs that are different from yours.

Data analysis usually starts out pretty hazy. The process of building a good data question and pairing it with good data sources is usually pretty messy. Give yourself permission to adapt the activity to your unique education role.

And last, remember that this process will get faster for you and eventually will become automatic and subconscious. But until then, I encourage you to invest in the time to take it slow while you build up your brain's muscle memory.

Step 1: Review the Elements of a Good Data Question

There are four elements to a good practical data question:

- ◆ They're directly connected to the decisions you need to make as an educator
- ◆ They're broad enough to require multiple sources of data
- ◆ They're specific enough to help you narrow down your data
- ◆ They're answerable on the right timeline

Step 2: Read Through the Example Scenario and Data Question

Example 1

♦ Scenario: Alexandra works at the district office. She coordinates Social Emotional Learning workshops for teachers in his school district. These workshops happen once a month.

♦ This is Alexandra's data question: Is the audience at my workshops learning and using the workshop content?

♦ Alexandra's available data: Sign-in sheets from past workshops and survey results.

Example 2

♦ Scenario: Marco teaches third grade. He's planning next week's math lessons.

♦ Marco's data question: Did the students learn how to use multiplication in a word problem this week?

♦ Marco's available data: last year's end of year scores, daily notes, anecdotal stories, quiz scores, and quarterly formative assessments.

Step 3: Discuss the Data Questions

Use these reflection questions to discuss the scenarios:

1. How well does this question connect to the person's day-to-day work as an educator?
2. Is the person's data question broad enough to require more than one source of data?
3. Is the person's data question narrow enough that they can focus only on the most meaningful data?
4. Which data sources will take too long to get? Which ones will arrive right on time?

Step 4: Improve the Question

Set a timer for 2 minutes. Each person in the group will write down one way they think the person can improve their data question. After time is up, each person will share. Finally, the group discusses the improvements and collaboratively improves the data question.

Note

1. I'm writing this in August of 2021. As I write, new cases of COVID-19 are rising again and schools all over the United States are trying to figure out if and how students should come back in-person. I hope that by the time you're reading this, things are much better and you're dealing with the more typical start-of-the-year stress from years past.

10

Practical Is Personal

In This Chapter

In this chapter, you'll learn how to

- ♦ Make data use practical by connecting your job duties, decisions, and data
- ♦ Learn about a mind shift that relieves stress and adds joy to your data use

Suggested Reflection

As you read this chapter, make the learning personal by answering these questions:

- ♦ How well do you think your daily activities align with the activities in your job description?
- ♦ Which decisions are the most important for your daily work?

DOI: 10.4324/9781003139751-13

♦ Are there any informal sources of data you use to make important decisions that would surprise your teammates?

Seneca, the Roman philosopher, said this sometime around AD 65: "If one does not know to which port one is sailing, no wind is favorable." Seneca was not an educator pondering practical data use in schools, but he sure offered sound advice for us seeking to do just that.

Think of the important decisions you make every day. These are your ports. And now think of all the data available to support you. These are the winds. If you don't know which decision you're making, no data is favorable.

In this chapter, we'll explore a technique for identifying your important decisions so the data you pick brings the most value to your students. And like Seneca, we can use our intentionality to get to our favored port. Ready to sail?

What Are Your Job Duties?

Take a moment to reflect on your workday. Think of the moments where you feel most in sync with your job duties. If you're a teacher, that might be delivering the lesson you planned a few days before. If you're a principal, it might be motivating the team during a staff meeting. If you're a school psychologist, it might be doing an evaluation with a student.

These are your core job duties. Sometimes they're tasks that appear on your job description. Other times they're the gritty and thankless tasks that are critical, but never appear on a job description. Either way, if you can't identify them, you might find yourself going through the motions of using data. It's the most discouraging kind of data practice—the kind done completely out of obligation. On the other hand, if you can name your core job duties, you're one step closer to making your data use meaningful (Figure 10.1).

Job Duty, Key Decisions, and Data

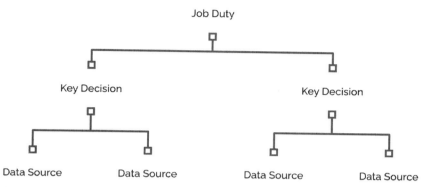

FIGURE 10.1 Practical is personal. Plan your data use so it connects directly to the decisions that are important for your work.

What Are Your Key Decisions?

Once you identify your core job duties, ask yourself "What are the most important decisions I make when I'm performing these job duties at the highest level?" If you're a teacher, that might be deciding on what content to reteach. If you're a principal, that might be choosing staff development for the next quarter. And if you're a school psychologist, that might be identifying a student's learning disability.

These are your key decisions. Identifying these is your next big step towards practical data use. That's because knowing your decisions helps you know what kind of data you'll need to make those decisions successfully.

For example, have a look at these core job duties, paired with a key decision. Here's what it might look like for a teacher (Table 10.1):

TABLE 10.1 Core Job Duties and Decisions (Teacher Example)

Core Job Duty	Decision
Differentiate instruction	Which students should go into small groups?
Teach math lesson	Which standard should I teach?

Here's what it might look like for a special education provider, like a speech and language therapist (Table 10.2):

TABLE 10.2 Core Job Duties and Decisions (Speech and Language Therapist Example)

Core Job Duty	Decision
Conduct speech evaluations	Which student should I evaluate first?
Plan speech goals for students	What's a reasonable learning goal for one year?

There are usually multiple decisions that go into a single job duty. But notice how getting really specific about even just one leads you to the next step, selecting your data sources.

What Are Your Data Sources?

Now that you've identified the decision you want to make, it's time to pick the data source to inform your decision. But how do you decide on which data sources to use?

Pick data sources that reflect the facts required to make your key decision. For example, a teacher might form small groups based on reading levels from an assessment. A district office administrator might pick professional development topics based on results from a survey about professional interests. A behavior specialist might decide the next step on a behavior plan based on two weeks of behavior charts.

Let's build on the chart that we used above and add a column for data sources and another column for how often we need them. Here's what this might look like for a teacher (Table 10.3):

TABLE 10.3 Core Job Duties, Decisions, and Data (Teacher Example)

Core Job Duty	Decision	Data	Frequency
Differentiate instruction	Which students should go into small groups?	Exit tickets	Every other week
Teach math lesson	Which standard should I teach?	Planning notes from grade level meeting	Quarterly

Here's what it might look like for a special education provider, like a speech and language therapist (Table 10.4):

TABLE 10.4 Core Job Duties, Decisions, and Data (Speech and Language Therapist Example)

Core Job Duty	Decision	Data	Frequency
Conduct speech evaluations	Which student should I evaluate first?	List of evaluations with due dates	Monthly
Plan speech goals for students	What's a reasonable learning goal for one year?	Baseline skill data and past goal progress	Quarterly per student

Each Decision Is a Hypothesis

At this point you've made some precise connections between your job duties, the important decisions you make every day, and the data that helps support those decisions. There's one more mind shift to make before we end this chapter. It's a subtle one, but trust me when I say it will relieve stress and encourage you to joyfully embrace the process.

That mind shift is this: the important decisions we make are experiments. And like all experiments, the only way for us to improve is to take our best shot, reflect on the result, and revise.

That reframe might feel a tad formal for your daily decisions because they happen so fast you sometimes don't notice them. As one interviewee told me, "When I first started teaching, sometimes I felt like I was just one chapter ahead of the students." But just as an academic researcher comes up with a theory to test, educators constantly come up with decisions to try.

So keep it casual—the point isn't to get it perfect. The point is to make better decisions. And to do that, you need a healthy dose of curiosity about what's working and what's not.[1]

Let's look at a hypothetical example of what I mean. Let's imagine Aaron, a teacher, wants to teach his students to articulate the purpose of their daily lessons. His professional intuition tells him he's got to change his approach. Consider this statement:

> *I reviewed my exit tickets and about a quarter of the students could not name the purpose of the lesson. I'll reteach tomorrow.*

And now consider an alternative statement, which takes a more curious tone:

> *I reviewed my exit tickets and about a quarter of the students could not name the purpose of the lesson. One reason for that might be that I didn't express the purpose clearly enough. Another reason might be that I didn't express the purpose enough times. I wonder if using a visual might help. And if that doesn't work, I can try again but with a smaller group.*

Notice the possibilities that open up when Aaron takes a more curious approach. And if something doesn't work, he's got other ideas waiting in the wings to try.

How does viewing our decisions as experiments relieve stress and help us experience this process with a little more joy? I believe that when we see our decisions as experiments, we let go of any perfectionist tendencies. That frees us to just get started. And when the decisions we make don't turn out the way we wanted, despite our best intentions, we know this is a step towards learning what will work.

Conclusion

When we use data practically in schools, it lives in tight integration with the various tasks, big and small, we do daily. And if we use data that doesn't directly support these tasks, it feels like a chore.

So as you progress along your journey towards increasingly practical and joyful data use, don't despair if it starts to feel a little meaningless. That's a signal that it's time to return to the exercise in this chapter and reconnect your job duties, key decisions, and data sources.

In the next chapter, we'll explore some ways to check-in on how your practical data experiment is going.

Activity: Making Meaning Out of Data in Three Steps

In this activity you'll learn to set up your data sources so they match your daily decisions and job duties.

How This Helps Us

We have so much data available to us that it can feel disconnected from our everyday work with students. It's not immediately clear how statewide testing data, reports from classroom software, and less formal data like meeting notes fit into our daily decision-making. But when we remember that practical data use is a means and not an end, we use our daily decisions as the guide for narrowing down our sources of data. When we coordinate our job duties, important decisions, and data, using data feels like an essential tool of our craft instead of a chore we do out of obligation.

Instructions

1. Identify one core job duty. A core job duty is something you'd find in your job description. For a teacher it might be preparing and delivering math lessons. For a school psychologist it might be writing reports to share assessment results. For a principal it might be delivering meaningful professional development.
2. Identify a key decision associated with this job duty. These are the decisions that, if you do them well, lead to success in your job duties. If you're a teacher, this might be deciding who goes into small groups for reteaching. If you're an occupational therapist, this might be selecting

the best writing tool for a student. Take note of how often you make this important decision. You'll need that for the next step.

3. Identify a data source that reflects the facts of the decision you picked in step two. Make sure you can get this data as often as you need to so you have fresh information when you need to make a decision. If you're a teacher, you might look at exit slips before organizing small groups. If you're a principal, you might look at staff surveys and notes from one on one meetings before planning professional development.

Note

1. I was surprised at how much research has been done on the role of curiosity in learning to do something new. There's way too much to summarize here, but for an example see Wade, Shirlene, and Celeste Kidd. "The role of prior knowledge and curiosity in learning." *Psychonomic Bulletin and Review*, no. 26, 2019, pp. 1377–1387.

11

Reflect and Revise

In This Chapter

In this chapter, you'll learn

- ♦ How to reflect on the outcome of your decision-making on your own
- ♦ How to reflect on the outcome of your decision-making with a teammate
- ♦ Three ways to get feedback on your data-informed decision that fit into your busy schedule

Suggested Reflection

As you read this chapter, make the learning personal by answering these questions:

- ♦ Where in your schedule can you find twenty minutes to reflect on data-informed decisions and how they've gone?

DOI: 10.4324/9781003139751-14

- Who is your go-to teammate who's great at giving constructive feedback?
- What can you do to let teammates know you're available to listen and give feedback on their practical data use?

While researching for this book, I spoke with Graciela, an elementary school teacher in a school in Southern California. Graciela is a seventeen-year veteran teacher who specializes in teaching students who are English and Spanish learners. As I listened to Graciela, I was struck by how much she owned the learning of her students. Underneath her stories was an unspoken question: how can I improve what I do for students? For Graciela, data helped her not only reflect on the student outcomes, but also on the effectiveness of her teaching.

Her conception of how it all works is shockingly simple. She expects herself to successfully teach all her students. So she uses data to check and see if that's happening. When data suggests that's not happening, she experiments with new ideas and checks again: "The data helps me see when some students didn't understand the lesson. When that happens, there's something about my teaching that didn't connect. And because of that the students didn't apply the skills. Once I know that, I can decide what to do differently."

Like all teachers who teach the way Graciela does, she eventually needs to see how well her plan is working. If you've been following along so far, you've learned how to connect your job duties, key decisions, and data sources into a chain of practical and data-informed decision making. Now it's time to put those connections to work in the real world and see how it's all turning out. Here are some ways to do that.

Reflect on Your Own

In the last chapter you learned to organize your data use by connecting your job duties, decisions, and data sources.

Organizing it in this way helps educators get clear on what's practical and what's not. It helps them avoid vague connections between what we're trying to accomplish and the evidence we use to support decisions.

Organizing your data use this way has another benefit: after you make a decision or decide on a next step, you can revisit your plan and reflect on the outcome. You already know how to check the outcome because you've picked sources of data that are connected to your key decision (see the previous chapter for more on this). Take a measurement using that data source again and see if your results have changed.

When we keep a record of our plans, it keeps us honest. That's because we tend to evaluate our decisions based only on how well the outcome turned out. Unfortunately, our brains tend to take the outcome and use it to fill in details about how we got there. When this happens, it makes it hard for us to learn from the experiences because we don't have an objective record of how we made the decision. This happens so often it has a name: hindsight bias.[1]

The Hypothesis

For example, imagine a school principal planning professional development for teachers at their school. The principal wants to choose content that's meaningful to the staff. Over three quarters of the staff mentioned behavior in a survey as an area they wanted to improve in. And the directors at the district office have been funding content on social emotional learning. So the principal decides to coordinate professional development that focuses on positive social behaviors.

The principal now has a hypothesis (for more on why decisions are like hypotheses, see the previous chapter). Here's how they might write this hypothesis in their data notebook:

Based on results from a staff survey and information about district level spending, positive social behaviors seems to be a meaningful topic for professional development.

The expert move here is deceptively subtle and thus easy to avoid: the principal has to write the theory down. Then they can reflect later on how well the teachers responded.

The Reflection

Ok, so the principal in our story believes positive social behaviors is the way to go with professional development. Fast forward eight weeks. Now the professional development is complete. It's time to go back to their theory and reflect. What data can they use to reflect on their theory?

Imagine that you are the principal in the story. If you organized the connection between job duties, key decisions, and data as discussed in the last chapter, you already have a data source. It's the same one you used to make the decision. Let's go back to our example to make this idea concrete.

Recall that the principal in our example used staff survey data and information about district spending to make their decision. They also wrote their hypothesis down in their data notebook, so they can hedge against the dreaded hindsight bias. Let's look at how they can use that same sentence to create a reflection and thus another decision point.

Here's the hypothesis:

Based on results from a staff survey and information about district level spending, positive social behaviors seems to be a meaningful topic for professional development.

. . . and now here's the reflection:

I can use a new staff survey and a phone conversation with a district director to reflect on my decision to focus on positive social behaviors.

These two sources of data—a staff survey and a phone conversation to get input—will give the principal new information to help guide what they do next. And since they've planned around the connection between their job duties (creating an environment where teachers grow professionally), related decisions (choosing staff development content), and data (surveys and district input), all these steps result in practical value in their work.

Reflect With Others

The legendary Zen monk Shunryū Suzuki said this about learning: "In the beginner's mind there are many possibilities. In the expert's mind there are few."[2] I love this quote because it reminds me how important it is to maintain the mentality of a learner, no matter how good we get at our craft. Then I think about how lucky I am that I work in public schools, because I'm quite literally surrounded by teachers.

Which brings us to the second technique for reflecting on our decisions: surround yourself with people who get what you're trying to do, then ask them for feedback.[3]

You can start by sharing your work with a teammate and asking them to react. For example, if your system for organizing small groups uses exit slips, show them how that connects to your key decisions. Maybe your teammate will say "I use exit slips just like that and it also helps me create small groups." Or maybe they'll say, "I use exit slips too, but instead of just reading them I enter them into a spreadsheet." Either way, all information is friendly to your mission.

The benefit of getting feedback also goes in the other direction. You might give your teammate inspiration for new data practices. When you show your teammates how your practical data use plan works—the connection between your job duties, important decisions, and data—you create the conditions to inspire. It's a service to them as much as their feedback is a service to you.

This is not a rigorous scientific process. That's ok, because we're not submitting to a scientific journal. Instead, we're looking to external influences to inform our decision making.

Reflecting With Others: Three Versions

In the first section of the book, you saw that learning to use data practically requires a precious resource educators rarely have, time. How can we find time to share our practical data plan with teammates?

Here are three ways to do this—a short version, a medium version, and a long version. Pick the one that suits your schedule, or modify any of the approaches to work better for you. The important thing is to include reflection and refinement as part of your process. Even doing this imperfectly is better than not doing it at all.

- ◆ Short: Email the key decision and data you're working on to a few teammates for feedback. I give an example email in the activity section below. If your teammates are used to giving and receiving feedback, consider starting an email thread for everyone to participate in
- ◆ Medium: Set up a thirty-minute meeting with one to two other teammates to share and discuss your practical data plans
- ◆ Long: Use time during a staff meeting to share how you're using data in small groups. I give example discussion questions in the activity section

Tim Brown, chair of the global design company Ideo, says this about the development of early ideas, or prototypes: "Prototyping is always *inspirational*—not in the sense of a perfected artwork but just the opposite: because it inspires new ideas."[4] How you use data is a work in progress, but expect to find wonderful new ideas along the way. When you reflect on how your plan is going and you share your process with teammates, you create the raw materials for innovation and improvement.

Conclusion

Remember Graciela, the teacher I wrote about in the introduction? She shared a story with me that exemplified what reflection and revision looks like in real life.

Graciela was reviewing reading assessment scores from the instructional software her school uses. She noticed a peculiar pattern. She looked at the data for time spent on each assessment item. The comprehension questions students answered incorrectly were also questions they spent the least time on. Graciela pondered this in a text message to me: "I realized that students were either rushing to answer the questions or they didn't understand them." I texted back, "Is there a way to tell which it is?" Her response was practical data use in action.

Graciela started by printing out an article to read and analyze as a class. That way, she could control the pace and spot any rushing. With her guidance, the students could follow a more methodical approach to working through the material. Then, she collected interview data from the students themselves: "It's the conversations that are powerful. The students tell us that they either struggled, weren't interested in the topic, or simply rushed to complete the task."

And that's the process in action.

Graciela thought about the assessment data, then developed her hypothesis. But she knew the assessment couldn't prove or disprove it. So she tried a new idea—slowly reviewing the material with the class—and gathered more data. Reflect and revise. Reflect and revise. Rinse and repeat.

Folks who work with me will tell you that I'm a strong supporter of planning, probably to a fault. And even I must admit that there's no amount of planning that replaces observing reality as a way to improve. There's no guarantee that how I use data and make decisions will turn out the way I hope, but I always know I'll learn from trying.

So as you keep plugging away, revising your own system for practical data use, be sure to include time to reflect on how things are going. Pat yourself on the back for trying, get back to the lab to come up with more ideas, then try again. And if you can build a crew of like-minded practical data users to come along for the ride, you just might change the way data is used at your school.

Activity: Reflecting on Job Duties, Decisions, and Data

What This Does

The purpose of this activity is to practice going back to key decisions and data choices for some reflection. After the activity, you'll have some new insights about how things turned out with your key decision and related data. Use the answers from your reflection to make improvements to your plan.

How This Can Help Us

Practical data use in schools is an iterative process. That means that we get better at it by trying something, reflecting on how it turned out, making some changes, and trying it again. Here's the attitude to take: be less of a perfectionist and more of a curious practitioner. Including reflection questions in your routine creates regular chances for improving your practical data use process.

Instructions

Chart your job duties, key decisions, and data sources in a document or on a piece of chart paper.

Use these questions to reflect on your practical data plan:

- ◆ Do I still believe this is the job duty I should be focusing my planning on right now? If not, which one?
- ◆ Do I still believe this key decision empowers me to perform this job duty well? If not, which one does?

♦ Do I still believe this data source empowers me to make this decision better? If not, what other data sources can I try?

Activity: How to Get Feedback by Email

What This Does
You'll learn to use an email template to get input on your practical data use plan.

How This Can Help Us
Time is always a barrier to our practical data use in schools. Any approach we pick to get better at this needs to be as efficient as possible. Using email to get input on your practical data plan can work in a pinch if you can't meet in person. It gives your teammate freedom to offer help when it suits their schedule. And as a bonus, it also requires you to write your ideas and questions, which forces an intentional approach to getting input.

Instructions
1. Write an email to get input on your practical data use plan. You can use the example below for inspiration.
2. In your email, include the job duty, decision, and data source you want input on. Be sure to also include your plan for analyzing how things turned out. Remember that both these plans often use the same data source.
3. Save this email in your drafts folder so you can update and send it quickly in the future.

Here's an example email to use for sharing your practical data use plan with teammates.

Hi, Briana. When you get a chance, would you be able to look this over and give me some input? It's a practical data use plan I put together for selecting this year's professional development.

Here's what I'm thinking for selecting the staff development content:

> *I can use a staff survey and input from school district directors to help me choose professional development that promotes student learning.*

. . . and afterward here's what I'm thinking to refine the process for next quarter:

> *I can use a staff survey and a phone conversation with a district director to reflect on my decision to use content on positive social behaviors as professional development.*

I'd love to hear what you think I could do better here. Let's swap ideas! I'm curious about what your process is like for planning staff development.

Maria
School Principal

Notes

1. Kahneman, Daniel. *Thinking, Fast and Slow*. New York, Farrar, Straus, and Giroux, 2011.
2. Suzuki, Shunryu. *Zen Mind, Beginner's Mind: 50th Anniversary Edition*. Shambhala, 2002.
3. From my own experience, I can't overstate how important collaboration is when working with data in schools. When you get really focused on a set of questions and you use your collective brain power to come up with new ideas, something close to magic happens. For more, see Lachat, Mary Ann, and Stephen Smith. "Practices That Support Data Use in Urban High Schools." *Journal of Education for Students Placed At Risk*, 2005, pp. 333–349.
4. Brown, Tim. *Change by Design, Revised and Updated: How Design Thinking Transforms Organizations and Inspires Innovation*. Harper Business, 2019.

Part 4
A New Direction

A few years ago, I was eating by myself at one of my favorite California hamburger restaurants. I've eaten at this restaurant many times, but on that day I noticed the French fries were unusually good. Like, stop-chewing-and-sit-with-it-for-a-moment kind of good. I continued enjoying this meal until a young man who worked at the restaurant came outside with a broom to tidy up the area. He casually asked, "How's the food tasting today?" I said, "This is not only the best version of your French fries I've tasted, but I'm having an internal debate about whether these are the best French fries I've ever had. Did you prepare them differently?"

The man stopped sweeping and said, "No, we cooked it the same way. It's not the cooking. Every morning we test the sugar levels of the potatoes. If the sugar levels don't pass the threshold, we can't use the potatoes. Most days the potatoes do pass the threshold. But on some days, like today, they exceed the threshold. That's why those fries taste so good."

Most fast food restaurants harvest potatoes during the time of year when they've got the most sugar. Then they freeze them until they're ready to be cooked. But at this establishment, they value fresh ingredients so much that they refuse to use frozen potatoes. They value it so much that they'd rather require a daily sugar test than freeze and store sugary potatoes.

What do you value most with data? And do you value it enough that you're willing to do things differently than before?

If the way data is used at your school doesn't feel practical, you'll need to head in a different direction. You can find your

DOI: 10.4324/9781003139751-15

own way, just make sure it's not back to what you used to do. This section is all about following that new direction. In the first chapter, you'll learn how to move away from the data-intuition false dichotomy and toward data use that brings more of yourself to the equation. And in the second chapter, you'll move away from meaningless data use and towards something that feels more connected to yourself and others.

Read this if:

♦ You believe that data-informed decision making inter-feres with gut-informed decision making
♦ You've been using data practically for a while, and are looking for ways to expand your practice
♦ You want to learn how to present data to an audience by making a connection with them

Activities in This Section

You'll find these activities at the end of each chapter in this section:

1. Combining Intuition and Data in Three Steps.
2. Data Presentation Worksheet.

12

When Intuition and Data Meet

In This Chapter

In this chapter I'll share stories to help you reframe how your intuition and reasoning work together, not against each other.

Suggested Reflection

As you read this chapter, make the learning personal by answering these questions:

- ♦ When was a time you thought using data required that you ignore your intuition?
- ♦ When was a time you thought paying attention to your intuition made you a worse data user?

It was a legendary battle of the scholars.[1] In one corner was Nobel Prize winning psychologist Daniel Kahneman, who championed the power of reasoning to overturn predictable errors in human judgement. And in the other corner was psychologist

DOI: 10.4324/9781003139751-16

and researcher Gary Klein, who argued that expert intuition was the key to unlocking excellence.

But the most interesting thing about these two seemingly opposing views wasn't the conflict, it was the resolution. In 2016, Klein and Kahneman co-authored an exploration of intuition brilliantly titled "Conditions for Intuitive Expertise: A Failure to Disagree."[2] In it, they moved past their intellectual differences to dig into the nuances of what makes intuition successful.

The story of Kahneman and Klein's unlikely collaboration could be a message about how we think about data use in schools: making decisions based on data and making decisions based on intuition aren't opposing approaches.[3]

Before we explore what this all means for practical data use in schools, let's ground ourselves in some definitions.

Intuition and Data: Definitions

I like this definition of intuition: "Quick and ready insight."[4] That's the rapid, almost magical, instinct we build up over our professional careers. We instantly know when students aren't their usual selves. We get tense during staff meetings if we feel a tough conversation coming. And when we coach new educators, we can observe and quickly spot the chances for improvement.

Now let's look at the other side, data. In this chapter, we'll use data, logic, and reasoning interchangeably. Here's a definition of reasoning I like: "the power of comprehending, inferring, or thinking especially in orderly rational ways."[5] This is the slower, logical style of thinking that we use to understand complex problems and find creative solutions. We use reasoning to weigh all the options before sending a sensitive email. We also use it when we look at student assessment results and identify patterns in errors.

Take a moment to reflect on which of these words resonates the most with you. Which do you find yourself relying on most during your workday? What if I told you a key to mastering data is to learn how to use both?

We Aren't Robots

In a previous chapter, I talked about my time at the Strategic Data Project, which is a program of the Center for Education Policy Research at Harvard University. I've got one more story about the Strategic Data Project, this time about a lesson I learned on data and intuition.

Spending time at the Strategic Data Project was like going to Hogwarts, except instead of learning magic with wizards I got to learn analysis skills with education data scientists. Days were spent writing code and studying theories of change. Evenings were spent deepening my relationships with my new friends. It was amazing.

During one activity, I was analyzing a school district's enrollment data. My assignment was to identify and quantify any relationships between a school's enrollment and a school's funding.

Like an earnest teacher's pet, I used every tool I learned: I carefully prepared the data. I calculated averages and ran tests. And I typed it all up in a written report.

I clicked the "submit" button for the assignment and waited for feedback from my instructor. It came a few days later and could be summarized like this: For all my attention to the technical details of the analysis, I left out the single most important thing. I didn't use what I knew as a former school psychologist and current administrator to explain what was happening in the data.

I missed the opportunity to marry my intuition with my reasoning. It's a connection that's crucial to practical data use because, as my instructor said on that day's feedback notes: "It's why we do our jobs and not robots."

Data and Intuition Are Our New Story

Up until that point, I told myself what I needed to use data better was more technical skills. It turns out what I was missing wasn't more statistics or coding skills, it was the connection between data and my real-life experience. This is the kind of experience that can only come from working in the field where that data itself is created.

During my time at the Strategic Data Project, I learned that I had separated data (an objective measure) from my experiences (subjective interpretations).[6] And, importantly, I learned that there's a whole new world of analysis to explore once I start using both together (Figure 12.1).

If we think of data and intuition as mutually exclusive, it's understandable that we'd have bad feelings about using data. We'd start seeing data as replacing our judgement, instead of supporting it.

Consider this statement:

The more data I use, the less I apply my own judgement.

Intuition and Data Work Together

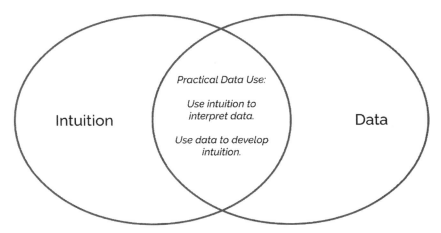

FIGURE 12.1 The relationship between intuition and data.

. . . and consider this reframe:

The more data I use, the better informed my judgement is.

The first statement minimizes your judgement. The second statement supercharges it.

Imagine these scenarios and notice how the educator keeps themselves in the driver's seat as they use the data to make decisions:

As a school psychologist: "These are my assessments by month across the whole year. Notice the increase in referrals near the end of each quarter. **Maybe there are a lot of concerns from teachers and parents right before grading? Let's ask around and see what we find.**"

As a teacher: "These are the quiz scores after we did the unit on Mayan civilizations. The average is lower than recent scores. I noticed a lot of hesitation during our conversations. **Maybe they need more support comprehending the text? Let me come up with some ideas to reteach.**"

As a principal: "These are the parent survey results from the last principal coffee talk. I noticed lower satisfaction scores on the communication section. **Maybe this has to do with the change we made to our parent email newsletter? Let's contact some parents to see if we can learn more.**"

In each of these scenarios, the data is there to point the educator towards an opportunity for improvement. Their intuition is there to guide them towards a good data question. And to answer that question, the educator goes right to the people that generated the data.

Data and Intuition: A Tale of Two Conferences

As a professional educator, I attend education conferences where I get to learn and network with other educators. Since I use a lot of data science tools, I also attend data conferences, where I get to learn and network with other data scientists. I like going to these conferences and making new friends over common professional interests.

After going to enough of these, I noticed a pattern: I talked to people differently depending on which conference I was at. For example, when I was at education conferences, I'd say things like, "We can't just make decisions from our gut. We need data to help us get around our blindspots. Afterall, we're only human."

But when I was at data science conferences, I'd say things like, "We can't just make decisions based on numbers. We need stories so the data means something to people. After all, we're all human."

Practical data use requires us to balance an analytic approach with a human touch. As human beings, we make sense of our work through the stories we tell ourselves and through the stories of others.

When I'm my most "education-ey," the story I tell myself is "I do this for students and teachers." When I'm my most "data-ey", the story I tell myself is "I do this because I'm devoted to the scientific method." But honoring the experiences of the school community and applying the scientific method are not mutually exclusive. I can use data in a human way and I can help other humans in a data informed way.

Is there another way we can talk about this that better describes what's happening in the real world? Is it possible these stories are not mutually exclusive, but indeed closely connected? Have a look at these statements and notice how they work with each other instead of against each other:

- I can't just go off my gut, I need data to help me get around my blindspots AND
- I need human stories to help me connect with people so the data means something AND
- I do this for students and teachers AND
- I do this because I'm devoted to the scientific method

When I see through the lens of data and intuition, I see a whole world of possibilities open up for how I can use data more practically.

But is it possible for us to scale that way of thinking to decisions for many people and for many students? To answer that question, let's turn to a story about a predictive data tool.

A Technical Tool That Aids Intuition

How can a data tool that uses a complex algorithm be designed so school counselors feel at home using it? That was the question Daniel Jarratt and his team at Infinite Campus, who developed a K-12 student information and learning management system, set out to answer when they built an early warning system to prevent school dropout.[7]

When I talked to Daniel, head of learning science technologies at Infinite Campus, I was expecting to hear lots about the development of the algorithm that predicts the likelihood a student would graduate from high school on time.

Instead, Daniel and I had an hour-long conversation about how they designed their data tool to be one that school counselors would actually use. I was struck by Daniel's focus on this problem. Every detail in the early warning system was designed to aid school counselors in their mission to give their students the best shot at graduating from high school.

Here's an example: Infinite Campus's data tool estimated a probability score of a student dropping out of high school. A probability score can be as low as 0 and as high as 100. The higher the number, the higher the estimated chance of dropping out. But Daniel and his team wanted something more intuitive for the school counselors.

After all, in schools we tend to equate higher numbers with a better outcome. Can you imagine how weird it would be if quiz scores ranged from 0 percent to 100 percent probability of *not* knowing the content? Students would come home proudly saying, "I got a 0 on my test today, yay! I think?"

The solution? Daniel reversed the scale so school counselors could intuitively interpret them: "Even though it's a dropout predictor we decided we wanted higher numbers to be good. We inverted and went from 50–150 so they wouldn't confuse it with anything else."

Daniel's team didn't stop there. They knew school counselors didn't just want to look at data, they wanted to help their students. So they linked student-level data to research-based interventions that improved the chances of graduation: "We tagged every risk factor with an intervention. Then we built intervention-specific models. They have an overall graduation estimate then they have other scores based on each intervention."

I was intrigued by the effort Daniel and his team put into understanding how school counselors wanted to use their tool. I had to know more, so I asked Daniel how they learned about what everyday educators needed from their product.

Daniel's answer was powerful but straightforward: they engaged educators frequently as they developed their software product. This included frequent check-ins with school counselors, traveling to customer schools, and speaking at conferences in cities where customers were using their data tool.

Here's an example of how Daniel and his team built a student list to aid school counselors' decision making about student check-ins:

"There were people whose responsibility was to individual students. We needed to provide a way to help counselors decide who to check in with each week. So we included a caseload list counselors could sort to help them decide who to visit with and check on."

Data tools aren't good only because of their underlying technology. If that were true, we could just pay technology companies to build our data systems, automate our decisions, and call it a day. The best data tools are designed to support the important decisions educators need to make, the ones their professional intuition guides them to every day.

And if that's true about data tools, it might also be true about data use in general. Let me explain more.

When Data and Intuition Connect in Everyday Life

Take a moment to reflect on activities you do on a regular basis, just to keep your life going. You manage finances, you drive a car safely to the store, or you check on your child when they say they're not feeling well.

Now imagine doing any of these without an external source of information to aid your decision-making. Try making a big purchase without looking at your bank account online. Or driving on the freeway without a speedometer. Or estimating your child's temperature without a thermometer. Without these sources of data to check our intuition regularly, our intuition would improve very slowly, if at all. On the other hand, repeated use of these data sources make our personal finance, driving, and parenting intuition even better as we learn more from them over time.

Assessment results are practical when they give us clues about how our lesson plan worked. As a result, we get better at knowing what good lesson plans look like.

Behavior observation notes are practical when they give us details about a student's behavior—how often it happens, how long it happens, and what the triggers are. As a result, we get better at making intuitive decisions about behavior.

Parent surveys are practical when they empower parents to tell us what they think and what they need. And as a result, we build stronger intuitions about how to serve our community well.

When data speaks directly to our mission for students, it does not replace our intuition.[8] Instead, it empowers us to use our intuition better.

Conclusion

Our intuition and our data use are better together than they are apart. Sure, there are folks who'd prefer to spend most of their day working with data (you can't see it, but I'm raising my hand). And there are people who avoid looking at it at all costs. But there's no need to trap either of these folks in a box where they can't grow.

We don't have to decide between going with our gut or crunching the numbers. We can use our gut to crunch the right numbers. And we can crunch the numbers to improve our gut.

Activity: Combining Intuition and Data in Three Steps

What This Does
In this activity, you'll learn to make data use practical by combining intuition and data.

How This Can Help Us
Bringing our professional experiences and knowledge to the data turns the numbers into actionable information. It helps us bring out the story in the data. It helps us get to the questions and decisions that matter for our students.

Instructions
Apply your knowledge and experience to your data use with these steps:

1. **Imagine the moment when the data was generated**. It might have been a student taking a quiz, a teacher taking a survey, or a principal observing a lesson.
2. **Ask yourself, what might have been happening when the data was generated?** You might answer with something like this: the student understood what they read.

Staff were worried after the meeting. Or the students used the visual schedule to figure out where to go next.

3. **Based on your answers to step 2, decide your next move**. The idea here is to try something new, then look again to see how it turned out. Here are some examples:

♦ For teachers, reteach a lesson and check the quiz scores
♦ For principals, try a new activity at a staff meeting, then ask a teacher how they felt after

Bonus: Over time, this exercise will help you come up with more accurate ideas for step 2. In other words, your professional intuition will improve.

Notes

1. Kahneman calls collaborations between two seemingly revival scholars "adversarial collaborations," which I find absolutely endearing. He shares more about his work with Klein in Kahneman, Daniel. *Thinking, Fast and Slow*. New York, Farrar, Straus, and Giroux, 2011.
2. Kahneman, Daniel, and Gary Klein. "Conditions for Intuitive Expertise: A Failure to Disagree." *American Psychologist*, 2009, www.fs.usda.gov/rmrs/sites/default/files/Kahneman2009_ ConditionsforIntuitiveExpertise_AFailureToDisagree.pdf. Accessed 22 July 2021.
3. See Kahneman, Daniel. *Thinking, Fast and Slow*. New York, Farrar, Straus, and Giroux, 2011 and more recently, this article on the work of Dr. Joel Pearson: Hooton, Amanda. "Sixth sense: the science behind intuition." *The Sydney Morning Herald*, 24 April 2021, www.smh.com.au/lifestyle/life-and-relationships/sixth-sense-the-science-behind-intuition-20210304-p577wm.html. Accessed 15 May 2021.
4. Merriam-Webster. "intuition" *Merriam-Webster*, www.merriam-webster.com/dictionary/intuition. Accessed 15 May 2021.

5. Merriam-Webster. "reason" *Merriam-Webster*, www.merriam-webster.com/dictionary/reason. Accessed 15 May 2021.

6. If you've ever felt this way, you're not alone. Researchers in Belgium explored the roles of intuition and data when teachers made decisions about grade retention. Vanlommel, Kristen, and Roos Van Gasse. "Teachers' decision-making: Data based or intuition driven?" *International Journal of Educational Research*, vol. 83, 2017, pp. 75–83.

7. For more on Infinite Campus's data tool, see Christie, S. Thomas, et al. "Machine-Learned School Dropout Early Warning at Scale." *12th Annual Conference on Educational Data Mining*, 2019. *Infinite Campus*, www.infinitecampus.com/pdf/Machine-learned-School-Dropout-Early-Warning-at-Scale.pdf. Accessed 14 May 2021.

8. *In his research, Gary Klein and David Klinger explore decisions made under pressure by* researching the decision-making process of firefighters. They highlight the importance of past experience in decision-making. Klein, Gary, and David Klinger. "Naturalistic Decision Making." *Human Systems IAC Gateway*, vol. XI, no. 3, 1991.

13

Go Deep, Go Wide, Go Out

In This Chapter

In this chapter, you'll learn how to

- ◆ Improve your data work by digging deeper
- ◆ Improve your data work by exploring wider
- ◆ Present your data to an audience in a compelling way

Suggested Reflection

As you read this chapter, make the learning personal by answering these questions:

- ◆ When was a time you indulged your curiosity by digging deeper into the data?
- ◆ When you dug deeper into the data, what did you learn?
- ◆ What opportunities do you have on a daily or weekly basis to share data with others?

DOI: 10.4324/9781003139751-17

Have you ever struggled to get the impact you want out of your data use at work and in your career? You'd be in good company. One of history's most significant scientists struggled to get the most out of the data available to them too.

William Welch was a physician at Johns Hopkins Hospital and Medical School in 1884. Welch was a widely regarded researcher. His most notable achievement was discovering the bacteria that causes gangrene, which was ultimately named Bacillus welchii, after him.[1] Later, in 1918, Welch would play a significant role in battling the H1N1 virus known as the 1918 pandemic, which killed an estimated 675,000 people in the United States alone.[2]

And yet in John Barry's book *The Great Influenza*, he argues that these accomplishments did not launch Welch into the ranks of history's greatest researchers.[3] That was because Welch did not go deeper on his chosen topic as his career continued. Further, Welch did not explain how his discovery fit into the larger field of medicine, or for that matter within other fields.

Two Ways to Get Unstuck

Of course, this is a book about practical data use in education, not epidemiology. But in my experience, going deep on a topic and finding connections between topics are exciting ways to engage data in schools. It feels a bit like wandering around in a forest, hopelessly lost. Then, just when I think I'll never make it out, I stumble into a sunlit clearing. Immediately, all kinds of possibilities for how I can do things differently in my work appear for my consideration.

These two skills, going deep on a topic and making connections across other topics, deepen our connection with our work. Let's go back to John Barry's book. He describes these analysis skills as "horizontal vision" and "vertical probing":

Horizontal vision allows someone to assimilate and weave together seemingly unconnected bits of information. It allows an investigator to see what others do not see and to make leaps of connectivity and creativity. Probing vertically, going deeper and deeper into something, creates new information. Sometimes, what one finds will shine brightly enough to illuminate the whole world. At least one question connects the vertical and the horizontal. That question is, "So what?"

"So what?" The answer to that question is the very answer that makes your data use practical. You might be required to look at reports from classroom literacy software on a weekly basis. But so what? You might receive weekly attendance reports from the district office. Or cumulative enrollment numbers. Or parent surveys. But so what?

Sometimes you find the answer by looking around and exploring more. For example, a teacher might learn a new quiz format for their math lesson by borrowing ideas from a colleague's language arts quiz. Other times, the answer lies in digging deeper, like when a teacher goes beyond today's assignments, looks at the last four weeks of assignments, and discovers there's a pattern of missing homework.

When all the solutions for practical data use feel stale and outdated, explore wider. That means exploring other topics and finding lessons that connect to your job duties and key decisions. You might discover something that feels fresh, innovative, and exciting.

When you feel like you don't know enough about a topic, dig deeper. This means getting focused on the single topic you're learning about. Look at current data, but check out past data as well. It might also mean looking at a different data source. Or it might mean collecting more data and then looking again. Going deeper on a topic gives you all the juicy details required to make nuanced decisions.

I do this all the time in my own data work. Nowadays, I rarely look at a single source of data. When a superintendent

TABLE 13.1 Examples of Digging Deeper and Exploring Wider

Examples of Digging Deeper	Examples of Exploring Wider
• Reviewing past data • Collecting more data • Looking at disaggregated data, like ones that show outcomes by student groups	• Exploring data collection techniques in other fields, like healthcare or finance • Observing how teammates use data and mining for inspiration or new techniques • Looking at data use from a different content area, data collection at the district office level, or data collection on publicly available data websites

or director at a school district asks me to find the number of students in special education this year, I dig deeper. I find the number of students in special education in each of the last five years. Why do this? Because the number of students in special education this year means nothing without context. But it does mean something if I know that number is lower, higher, or the same compared to past years. Going deeper gets me there.

When you use data at work and it feels like there's something missing, try getting yourself unstuck by digging deeper or exploring wider. You just might find the spark you need (Table 13.1).

You won't be done with your data work yet though. After you meet the challenge of going deeper or exploring wider, you'll encounter a new challenge: you'll need to go out into the world and find a way to weave all these data sources into a narrative you can share with others.

How to Share a Data Analysis

The first time I put someone to sleep with a data presentation was sometime in the early 2000s. I was a school psychologist in a Southern California elementary school. One of my duties as a school psychologist was to administer tests to students, then decide if they had a learning disability.

This process required endurance from all involved—some from me, but more from others. Sadly for the student, this meant taking a lot of tests, as you might imagine given the importance of the decision. And sadly for the staff and parents, this meant enduring a presentation of all my findings and related data. That's a lot of findings.

At one such meeting, I was in the middle of reading out the results from a third psychological test when, from the corner of my eye, I noticed the most profound stillness coming from the other side of the table where my teammate sat. At first, I thought my teammate was transfixed by the thoroughness of my reporting. I looked in their direction. That's when, on closer inspection, I saw that my teammate was not deep in focus, but rather deep in what looked to be a much-needed nap.

I've hypnotized my audience into sleep a few times after this first incident, so I've had a lot of time to think about why it happens. In short, I learned that I can't present data in the same order that I analyze it.

Present in the Reverse Order That You Analyze

Generally speaking, here's how I analyze data from different sources:

1. First, I explore as many sources of data as I can.
2. Next, I find themes that come up across the data. Sometimes I see that a student group has different outcomes from other student groups. Or I see that participants at staff development events prefer shorter sessions.
3. Next, I think hard about if and why this theme is interesting or helpful. I ask questions like "Are the school leadership aware that some student groups benefit from their system more than others?" and "How would I do staff development differently if I knew the audience wants shorter sessions?"

4. And finally, I shape all of what I've learned in a story that is easy to share at a meeting.

The order of these steps makes for a great way to analyze data because they force me to start with lots of information, then discover specific patterns based on the evidence.

But as good as this sequence is for analysis, I've learned it's a rather inconsiderate way to present to an audience. That's because the part the audience really connects with, the story, is at the end. And if I'm presenting to an audience for whom data is not fun, they're going to need to sit through a lot to get to that story. It's a bit like inviting the audience to dinner at my house, but making them sit through a pitch for time-shares before wheeling out the shrimp cocktail in the last five minutes. Not cool.

So let's consider the reverse order:

1. First, I tell the story. When possible, I try to include characters, details, and a special moment where I learned something new.[4]
2. Next, I share why the story is interesting by pointing to the theme I discovered during my analysis.
3. And finally, I share one or two data points as examples of evidence. This brings some rigor to the theme and helps build credibility.

A note on preparation: I almost always come to my presentations with more data points than I need, in case the audience wants more (most of the time, they're happy with the one or two data points). Since I discovered the theme by exploring the data points themselves, I usually have a lot of data points to choose from.

So that's it. A simple reversal of the steps leads to a completely different emotional effect. Analyze lots of data to arrive at the story. Then, share with people by leading with a story and arriving at a few key data points.

Conclusion

Learning to use data in practical ways is a never-ending journey. Even after twenty years of working with school data, I'm still finding new ways to do things, learning from others, and enjoying the ride. That's because part of what makes data use practical is not making data the goal. Instead, make data the means to some other end that is larger than itself.

Use the practices in this chapter to explore how your practical data use can take you to an end that is larger than the data. If you're passionate about a topic, be it teaching math, organizing professional development, improving school systems, or social-emotional well-being, use data as a tool for going deep. Then look across a wide range of experiences and people. Explore and discover interesting and unusual connections. This will bring relevance to your specialization and will define how you contribute to the education community. And finally, share with others in compelling ways. Share with others in human ways. The data can't make connections with others for you. Only you can do that.

Activity: Data Presentation Worksheet

In this activity you'll learn how to organize and structure your data presentation into a compelling story for your audience.

How This Helps Us

When we analyze data, we start by collecting as much information as we can, then finding themes. In other words, we start with the numbers. But when we present data to an audience, starting with the numbers makes it hard for the audience to connect with you as a person and to the important information you're about to share.

Instructions

Prepare your data presentation like this:

1. Pick a theme or pattern that emerged from your data.
2. Select 1–2 examples from your data that illustrate the theme. You'll have many examples (that's what makes it a theme), but just pick 1–2.
3. Write a five-sentence story about how you see this theme in real life. Make it relatable by including characters, details, and something you learned.
4. Assemble your presentation in this order: story, theme, data point.

Here's an example, using my experience presenting testing results as a school psychologist (Table 13.2).

TABLE 13.2 Data Presentation Worksheet (Example)

Presentation Structure	What to Do	Example
1. Tell a story	Include characters, details, and important moments	Sharing a special moment when the student gave an interesting and informative response to a test
2. Share a theme	Share a pattern you found in the data	Explaining that the student seemed to excel in content with a lot of visual stimuli
3. Share a data point	Select 1–2 data points that illustrate the pattern well	A score from the test of visual perception, compared to a score from the test of auditory perception

Notes

1. Johns Hopkins Bloomberg School of Public Health. "William Henry Welch, MD." *Johns Hopkins Bloomberg School of Public Health*, www.jhsph.edu/about/history/heroes-of-public-health/william-henry-welch.html. Accessed 2 July 2021.
2. Centers for Disease Control and Prevention. "1918 Pandemic." *Centers for Disease Control and Prevention*, www.cdc.gov/flu/

pandemic-resources/1918-pandemic-h1n1.html. Accessed 2 July 2021.
3. Barry, John. *The Great Influenza: The Epic Story of the Deadliest Plague in History*. Penguin Books, 2005.
4. These story components are from Hall, Kindra. *Stories That Stick: How Storytelling Can Captivate Customers, Influence Audiences, and Transform Your Business*. HarperCollins Leadership, 2019.

Conclusion

Why Bother?

Congratulations. We've made it all the way through our education data journey together. I hope you found something validating, heart-warming, and useful in these pages. I'll leave you with one last story. And it's a personal one.

A few weeks before the manuscript for this book was due, my friend Heather asked me what turned out to be a profoundly important question: "Why do you like writing about data?"

As soon as I heard the question, my mind and body felt relaxed. It was the kind of relaxation one feels when they read a quote that delivers a punchline so profound they need to stop and sit with it. So that's what I did. And my mind drifted back about twenty years.

In my twenties, I doubted myself a lot. It was the decade of my life where all the imagined certainties of childhood evaporated. And in their place was the wondrous and threatening realization that my decisions were now truly mine to make. And just like that, my search for certainty began.

That time in my life presented many questions to fuel the search. Did I really have enough money in the checking account or is that just what I wanted to believe? Did I really want to go into school psychology or was I just avoiding going back to school for a Ph.D.?

Data became the external source of information that offered me some semblance of certainty. Not sure about the balance in my checking account? I could go online and check. Not sure if going into school psychology was the right choice? I could take a poll among my friends. But ultimately, I found that few things in life were one hundred percent certain, no matter how much twenty-seven-year-old me wanted them to be.

DOI: 10.4324/9781003139751-18

When this book hits shelves, I will have just turned 46. Data means something different now. I'm beginning to embrace the joy of life's basic uncertainties. In fact, uncertainty has become a kind of motivation. What if I write stories about data and the readers don't like it? They might not. But they also might.

And if I can't know for sure, why not write the book about data that I've always wanted? One with feeling, emotion, and in touch with reality. One that insists on marrying logic with intuition, thinking with feeling, and numbers with emotion. One that proposes that data should be a means for excellence instead of a means for punishment.

So the answer to my friend's question is that I write about data because I love doing it, and that's just fine. Put another way, in my twenties, data was a way to calm my worry that I wasn't good enough. In my forties, being good enough became the reason why I write about data.

That leads to my final piece of advice on how to make all this practical. I want to end by asking you to take a step back and have a look at the big picture. What's the thing you love about your education job? How can you relentlessly search for a way to express that in your work, no matter how impractical others say it is?

For me, that thing is helping educators use data. It might be something different for you, but whatever it is, I believe you can find a way to meaningfully incorporate it in your job. When you do that, not only will you find deeper meaning in your profession, but your students will see what it looks like when a grown up loves their work.

And in the big picture, that might be one of the most practical things of all.

Appendix A

More Content

Thank you for reading *The K-12 Educator's Data Guidebook: Reimagining Practical Data Use in Schools*. I hope you learned as much from it as I did while writing it. And I hope I've delivered on my goal to make a resource you'll want to keep in your briefcase or office as you discover what practical data use means for you.

I'm passionate about education and I enjoy writing about the real-life issues that influence the work of educators, be it data or otherwise. If that sounds interesting to you, consider checking out more of my work at my website.

And while you're there, I invite you to sign up for my email newsletters. I share activities, tips, stories, resources, and books I'm reading with subscribers.

The remaining appendices are bits and pieces of information that I thought would be helpful, but didn't quite fit into the main narrative of the book. I hope they help extend your learning.

For more information, visit my website at https://ryanestrellado.com

Appendix B

More Activities

What follows are more activities for you to try as you progress on your journey towards practical data use. I hope you find them useful. Feel free to use these and make modifications to suit your needs. And if they help you, I'd love if you shared your story with me by contacting me at my website, https://ryanestrellado.com.

Keep a Data Notebook

What This Does
This activity encourages you to journal as a way to practice recognizing and acting on your professional curiosities.

How This Can Help Us
As an educator, you have excellent judgement about what your students need. This judgement leads to meaningful data questions. Should we reteach a lesson tomorrow? Who needs to be in my small reading group? Are attendance rates consistent across schools? These are the kinds of questions that come up for you based on your professional experience. But you can't turn these questions into actions unless you notice and document them.

When you read through data, there's a quiet inner voice dialoguing. Sometimes that inner voice makes statements, like "I didn't expect that reading score to be so low." Other times the voice asks questions, like "Does this report include pre-school students?" This is your curiosity talking. Train yourself to notice and to follow it. Your data notebook is where you'll capture these curiosities for future research.

Instructions

Keep a data notebook. When you're curious about how things are going for your students, write yourself a note in the form of a good data question (see the chapter "Using Data Questions" for more on how to do this). Leave some space on each page so you can jot down more notes once you review some data.

Set aside a time every week to leaf through your data notebook. Still curious about some of the questions you've written? Start researching and see if you can find some answers. Here are some ways to follow-up on what you've written down:

◆ **Internet Searching Is Your Friend:** Whenever I'm curious about findings from a research paper or how to best interpret a graph, I start searching the internet. It's not always a complete solution, but it's almost always a great start.

◆ **Consult With Your Network:** Get to know the interests and expertise of your colleagues. Invite them to share their point of view with you on the questions you've written in your data notebook.

◆ **Observe People Who Are a Few Steps Ahead of You:** Similarly, identify people in your network that have experience with practical data use. Maybe they're great at finding, reading, and sharing research. Or maybe they know how to make pivot tables in spreadsheet software. If you see that skill in your future, start observing their methods and ask them lots of questions. Jot these insights down in your data notebook.

◆ **Find a Research Paper About the Topic You Wrote About:** Again, the internet is great for finding research. Try reading a research paper all the way through, even if you don't understand everything. Then pick a section and read it until you understand it. If you're like me, this method will generate new questions you'll want to pursue. Write these down in your data notebook.

Helpful Questions to Ask Before Trying Something New With Students

What This Does

In this activity, you'll learn questions to ask while planning new ideas for your students.

How This Can Help Us

As an educator, you get a lot of opportunities to try new things in your practice. Maybe your school is adopting a new Social Emotional Learning curriculum. Or maybe your school is trying new literacy software. Sometimes, it's something smaller, like a new weekly quiz format you want to try for your math lessons. To keep things student-centered, use these questions to stay data-informed and plan for any outcomes you'd like to avoid.

Instructions

Use these questions when you see patterns in your classroom data and get inspired to try something new with your students.

- ◆ What does this data tell us?
- ◆ What does this data not tell us?
- ◆ Does the data suggest something new to try with my students?
- ◆ How do I minimize the downside to my students if I try something new and it doesn't work out?

Team Conversations About Data

What This Does

You'll learn how to use a routine for sharing and developing different perspectives on data.

How This Can Help Us

We have a powerful tool for expressing our points of view and discovering new ones: conversations with our teammates. When we look at data, clarify our interpretation of it, and share with others, we seize an opportunity to discover new takes on the information. This process, when repeated and habituated, helps us improve our collective intuition about data interpretation in ways that are impossible when we do it on our own.

Instructions

Look at data with your teammates during a meeting. Before discussing, each participant should write down the answer to these questions on a sheet of paper:

- ◆ What does this data tell me?
- ◆ What does this not tell me?
- ◆ What am I not sure about?
- ◆ How can I learn more?

After each participant writes their own answers down, each will take a turn sharing what they wrote.

Lead with curiosity and talk about the answers together. End the activity by deciding on a collective action item based on the data.

Multiple Sources of Data

What This Does

In this activity, you'll practice using multiple datasets to learn more about a topic.

How This Can Help Us

This exercise helps us get out of the "Which dataset is correct?" conundrum. You know the one I mean. It's when two data sources measure the same thing but suggest different results. Sometimes we believe that means one must be wrong. But not always.

Salt is delicious. Caramel is delicious. But there was a time when these two ingredients weren't thought of as complimentary.

Someone had to put them together and see what that was like. It's the same thing with data.

Assuming that the sources of data have similar quality, we can see multiple data sources as an opportunity to understand a topic better. When we start working with multiple datasets, we bring more nuance to the way we understand what's happening in our classrooms.

Instructions

Take charts, tables, and reports from two different sources. For example, you can use two different assessments or quizzes that measure the same standard. Challenge yourself to write one sentence that summarizes all of the data. Then ask yourself:

- What does this data tell me?
- What does this not tell me?
- What am I not sure about?
- How can I learn more?

I Know a Student . . .

What This Does

In this activity, you'll ask questions about data that help you connect the data back to the stories of your students. Use these questions and sentence frames as part of your data meetings, your own data analysis, or during a personal reflection.

How This Can Help Us

The more we work with data, the easier it is for us to lose the connection between data and people. Managing and analyzing a lot of data can start to feel like its own job. To keep things grounded, it's helpful to have routines that remind us who generated the data in the first place—our students.

Instructions

Find a chart or table that has data about students. Identify all the elements of the chart or table using the techniques described in the Your Data Field Guide section. Then, try these sentence frames and questions out on your own or in a group discussion:

◆ This reminds me of a student I know. Their story is _____

◆ This doesn't remind me of my own students, but it does raise a question about them. That question is _____

◆ How would this chart or table look if it were about my students?

A Routine for Data Meetings

What This Does

You'll learn a straightforward routine for data meetings that includes exploring data, getting relevant information from it, and taking action.

How This Can Help Us

It feels overwhelming to be at a meeting, in front of tables, graphs, reports, or research papers, and not quite know what to do with all that. I've seen my fair share of meetings start with interesting conversations about the data, only to end without a clear action or summary of what was learned.

Having a routine empowers us to hold ourselves accountable for consistent review, discussion, and action using the data we have available.

Instructions

1. Take 10 minutes to answer these questions about a data-set on your own:

   a. What does this tell me?

   b. What does this not tell me?

    c. What am I unsure about?

    d. How can I learn more?

    e. Which students seem to be benefiting from my current plans?

    f. Which students don't seem to be benefiting from my current plans?

    g. What's something I can try differently tomorrow?

2. Take 10 minutes to share and discuss with a partner.
3. Write all the ideas for things to try tomorrow on a separate document.
4. Pick one idea to try before the next meeting.
5. At the next meeting, discuss how the changes went. Participants should present evidence to support their claims.
6. When the group needs to abandon an idea and try another, they can use the list they made in step 3 for the next idea to try.

Set Up Your Data Satellites

What This Does

You'll learn to create a checklist to use for making a key decision in your everyday work.

How This Can Help Us

You've got lots of decisions to make every day. For the ones that need to be data-informed, you need a way to jump into the data review and make a decision efficiently. Without clear steps, you risk recreating your process each time you make a decision. With clear steps, you'll get in and out of the decision quickly so you can do what really matters: being the awesome educator you are for your students.

Think of your data sources as little satellites. They collect information for you to review and use to support your key decisions. Now all you need is a procedure to follow so you can use what they've collected for you efficiently.

Instructions

Make a checklist. The first two to three items on your checklist should be trusty sources of data that you can get reliably. These are your little satellites, collecting information for you so you're prepared to make a decision when the time comes (for more on picking practical data sources, see the chapter "Practical is Personal"). The last item of your checklist should be a question that triggers an intuitive decision, informed by the data. Here's an example:

Example: Checklist for Monitoring Reading Lessons
1. Review notes from today's classroom reflection.
2. Review last week's reading quiz results.
3. Review scores from this week's literacy software assessment.
4. Ask myself, "What did I learn from this review? Do I need to change my teaching plans tomorrow?

Script for a Data Request Email

What This Does

This framework for data requests helps you construct your requests clearly, so the person you're asking understands what you need.

How This Can Help Us

On occasion, my coworkers ask me for help on doing something in a spreadsheet. I'm happy to help, so I always model the dark secret to data tool work: looking the problem up on the internet.

And so I helped my teammates that way for a long time—searching for solutions on the internet together and then trying them out. Eventually I noticed that they'd still ask me for help on their spreadsheets instead of feeling empowered to look the question up on their own. I realized what the problem was when one of my teammates told me "I'm not even sure I know the right question to ask."

So now I think a lot about how we can feel more confident about asking for help or looking for data. Having a framework for how to ask for data, along with some examples, can help you practice and develop a routine for data requests. Here's something you can use when you want to ask someone—a teammate, principal, or data analyst—for help finding data.

Instructions

Construct your email using these guidelines:

◆ What are you trying to learn?
◆ What's your data question?
◆ What data do you have? Why is it incomplete?
◆ What data would help you learn more about your students?

Here are some examples:

Example 1: Equity Analysis About Autism Services

[What are you trying to learn?]
Hi Joan! Hope you're doing well. Hey I'm working on a project with the folks on the Autism support team. We're putting together information about how often families in our community are using Autism-related services if they have a student in their family with Autism. These are school-based services like speech and language services, behavior support, or consultations with the family.

[What's your data question?]
Here's the main question for us: when we disaggregate the data by student groups, do we see different rates of service use?

[What data do you have? Why is it incomplete?]
We have a lot of this data from our online special education system. But there are a couple variables I'm not sure about. The first is special education program. We don't have a column that

tells us what kind of special education classroom each student participates in. Right now we're using the "time in general education classroom" variable as a clue about which program each student is in. But that can be misleading.

[What would help you learn what you want about your students?] Do you have any data we can use that helps us compare the number of students in each special education program?

Example 2: Planning Tomorrow's Lessons

[What are you trying to learn?]
Hi Marie! I'm building a planning routine to help me decide which students need to spend time with me in small groups every day.

[What's your data question?]
Here's the main question for me right now: which students didn't understand the math lesson?

[What data do you have? Why is it incomplete?]
Right now I've got weekly math quizzes that I look at. These help because I can sort my list by the number correct and select students from there. But I feel like that's not the whole picture—I want to know more about patterns in errors that my students are making. That will help me plan better for the small groups.

[What would help you learn what you want about your students?] Do you have any ideas for how I can get at that data better? Do you know of anyone I can talk to or observe who's got a good system for this?

Quantifying Your Observations

What You'll Learn
In this activity, you'll learn how to quantify observation or conference data.

How This Can Help Us

Educators get good information from data sources that aren't easily quantifiable, like meetings, conferences, and observations. Sometimes, notes from these events are good enough for making the decisions you face every day.

But since our notes are usually about one student, they limit how well we can see the big picture. When time allows, it's useful to quantify what we've learned so we can look at more data at once. This equips us to zoom out a level, and plan for more students.

Instructions

1. Find a source of data that you want to quantify. Some examples include notes from classroom observation, notes from student conferences about project work, or exit slips with open-ended prompts.
2. Identify the decision you need to make. Some examples include, "Do I reteach for the whole class or in a small group?" or "How should I assign students to groups during collaborative work time?"
3. Identify at least one criterion that helps you make this decision. Phrase the criterion as a question. Some examples are "Was the student able to summarize the reading passage?" or "Did the student use logical points to support their claim in their writing sample?"
4. Make a table where the first column is the name of the student and the next columns are the criteria from step 3 (Table 16.1).
5. Write a "1" in the cell next to the student and below each criteria if the student met the criteria and a "0" if they didn't. These are not grades and should not be shown to the student.

Once you have data for all your students, you can interpret it for decision-making. Here are examples interpretations:

TABLE 16.1 Quantifying Observations With a Table

Student	Summarized the reading passage?	Used logical points to support claim?
Frank	1	0
Sofia	0	1
Briana	1	1
Alex	1	0
Percent	75%	50%

In each column, find the percent of students who met a criteria. If that number is above a predetermined threshold you may choose to reteach in a small group. If that number is below the threshold, you may choose to reteach the whole class. For example, if more than half the students felt confused based on exit slip prompts, reteach to the whole class.

You can also use the dataset to group students. For example, you may want groups of four students, where each group has two students that met the criteria and two students who did not meet the criteria.

Lead Data Presentations With a Story (Includes Examples)

What This Does

This is a variation on the process for presenting data I wrote about in the chapter "Go Deep, Go Wide, Go Out."

This activity will help you plan your data presentation with a focus on connecting with your audience. Use it at data meetings, presentations, or meetings with parents.

How This Can Help Us

As practical users of data, we examine many data points. Then we synthesize those data points to draw conclusions. And last, we communicate what we found to an audience so we can make decisions together.

In most cases, it's not necessary to share every step of that process with our audience. In fact, I don't advise that you do, unless you want to help cure your audience's insomnia. This activity will help you plan your data presentation so you get your point across without reviewing every data point.

Instructions

1. Review all your sources of data. These could be classroom observation notes, quiz scores, survey results, reporting from instructional software, and other things.
2. Identify themes. A theme is an idea that appears across different sources of data. Here are some examples: "Some students struggled with the fraction lesson," or "Our homework policy is a hot topic."
3. If you have more than one theme, pick one to share.
4. And last, construct your sharing like this:

   - Tell a short story that illustrates the theme
   - Reflect on what you learned
   - Share one to two example data points that illustrate the theme
   - Talk about next steps

Here's an example: Let's say you're a principal and you need to share concerns about the homework policy at your school. You have these sources of data to draw from: parent surveys about the homework policy, observations of students grading homework, and interviews with teachers. Notice how the principal in the example shares two data points, not all of them.

1. **Tell a short story that illustrates the theme**: "Last Tuesday, I was talking to Jordan, a student in Mr. Duarte's class. I asked him how he was doing. He told me homework has been tough lately."
2. **Reflect on what you learned**: "This got me thinking about how long it's been since we've talked about our homework policy as a team. I've looked at a lot of information and I think there's an opportunity for us to improve it."

3. **Share why you think this might be happening**: "There's been feedback about how tough homework is. Maybe this has to do with how much we're sending home."

4. **Share one to two example data points from step 1**: "Let's look at our parent survey results as an example. More than 40 percent of the parents said they disagreed or strongly disagreed with the statement, 'The amount of homework is manageable for my child.' And another example: a few of you shared with me that the homework assignments being returned aren't completed."

5. **Talk about next steps**: "Let's brainstorm ways we can lessen the homework while still providing a good opportunity for the students to practice what they've learned. Then we'll look for volunteers to try some of the ideas and report back."

Appendix C

Additional Tips and Examples

There's something about reding or hearing examples that really brings new concepts home. What follows are additional tips and examples of how I've used data, reasoned with it, and talked about it. These are imaginary examples, but I wrote them to resemble the kinds of data you see in the education field.

Tips for Using Charts

Tips for using charts:

♦ Get as much information as you can from the title, sub-title, axis labels, and annotations. Data visualizations, when done well, combine words with pictures. They tell you about the data you're looking at and give hints about patterns

♦ Focus on comparisons. For example, use the length of bar charts to compare quantities across categories.

♦ If one of the axes contains dates or time, compare quantities over time. For example, use the height of the line in a line chart to see changes in enrollment over time.

Example 1: Bar Graph

One way to talk about it: "Each bar represents the percent of students that performed in the proficient range or higher in each grade level. There isn't one grade that stands out from the rest, but there's a pretty big difference between the third grade and fourth grade. Could be random, could be something different happening. Let's explore it" (Figure 17.1).

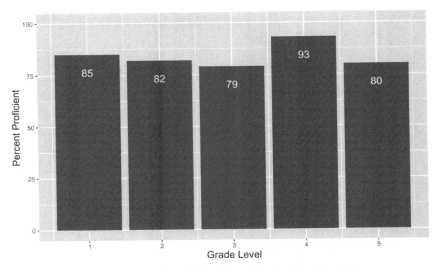

FIGURE 17.1 Percent of Students Who Scored in the Proficient Range

Source: Formative assessment data from first through fifth graders.

Example 2: Line Chart

One way to talk about it: "Each point represents the number of times Frank blurted out in class. The x-axis represents calendar days. When we look across time, March 4th stands out. I wonder what happened there? We started this behavior plan a week ago. Let's talk to Frank's teacher to see if they're noticing any difference" (Figure 17.2).

Example 3: Stacked Bar Chart

One way to talk about it: "The x-axis represents the grade level of the students who took this assessment. The y-axis represents the percent of students who performed at each proficiency level. Each color represents a proficiency level. When we look across grade levels, we see some differences in the number of students who might have struggled with this assessment. Let's look at the assessment responses and see if we can find patterns to address in reteaching" (Figure 17.3).

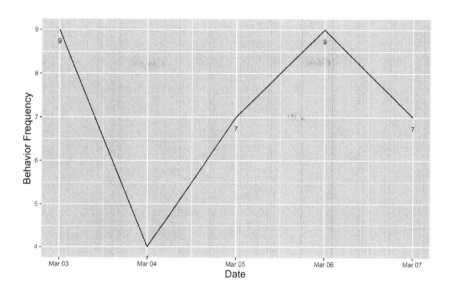

FIGURE 17.2 Behavior Frequency Over Time

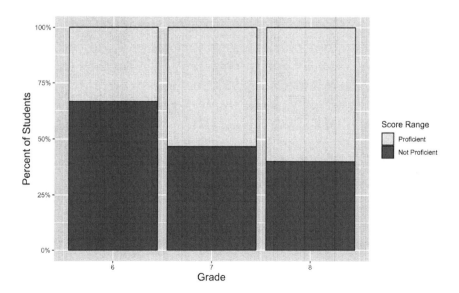

FIGURE 17.3 Formative Assessments by Grade

An Example of Using a Table

Try these questions to help you understand the data in a table:

- ◆ Each row in the data table is a _____.
- ◆ Each column in the data table is a _____.
- ◆ I can use this table to compare _____.
- ◆ These comparisons can help me make decisions about _____.

Here's an example. Imagine a teacher-made table that contains data about a classwork assignment worth 5 points, a homework assignment worth 10 points, and a quiz worth 100 points (Table 17.1).
Try the sentence frames to practice using the table:

- ◆ *Each row in the data table is a* _____. "Each row in this table is a student in my classroom."
- ◆ *Each column in the data table is a* _____. "Each column in this table is an assignment score. Each assignment is worth a different number of total points. There is a column for this week's classwork, homework, and quiz."
- ◆ I can use this table to compare _____. "For each student, I can look left and right and compare scores across each assignment." You might also make this observation: "I can't directly compare scores across assignments because each assignment is worth a different number of total points. I can fix this by turning each score into a percent of the total points for each assignment."

TABLE 17.1 Student Assignments (Example)

Student	Classwork	Homework	Quiz
Frank	4	9	75
Sofia	3	5	90
Edward	5	6	82
Jocelyn	2	3	63

◆ These comparisons can help me make decisions about
_____. "If I could compare the quiz score across all stu-
dents in my classroom, I can split them into three groups
based on this score. Then I can assign them to similar
groups for reteaching tomorrow."

Examples for Talking About Student-Level Data

If we can talk about our data, we can share it with each other.
And if we can share with each other, we can collaborate together.
Here are some examples of how I've talked about student-level
data in my own work:

"In last week's fraction assessment, I noticed many of my
students making similar errors. Here's one representative
example, Sarah's work sample."

"On average, students in foster care have a lower
attendance rate compared to students who are not in foster
care. We looked through the student-level data and identified a number of reasons why this is. For example, one
student has severe medical needs, so she misses school a
lot for doctor's appointments and hospitalization."

"We noticed a handful of students in our grade level
who did really well on the reading assessment. We looked
into what their day was like and saw that most of them
had been participating in small groups sessions at least
once a week. We'll be asking them how that's going to
see if we can get more clues about what's working."

Examples for Talking About Accountability Data

Here are some examples of how I've talked about accountability
data in my own work:

"Based on last year's end-of-year testing data, our school
fell into the blue zone, which is the highest possible

classification. We know from our state education agency's dashboard documentation that the color coding is based on the most recent test results and the results from last year. But let's look at our student-level data and groups to describe this result better."

"Based on our district's discipline data, the suspension rate for our Native American and African American students is higher than all other groups. Let's do a random selection of discipline events and see if we can understand what kinds of practices are creating these results."